T0305893

HCMBOK®
The Human Change Management Body of Knowledge

Third Edition

Best Practices and Advances in Program Management Series

Series Editor
Ginger Levin

RECENTLY PUBLISHED TITLES

The Human Change Management Body of Knowledge (HCMBOK®),
Third Edition
Vicente Goncalves, Carla Campos

Creating a Greater Whole: A Project Manager's Guide to Becoming a Leader
Susan G. Schwartz

Project Management beyond Waterfall and Agile
Mounir Ajam

Realizing Strategy through Projects: The Executive's Guide
Carl Marnewick

PMI-PBA® Exam Practice Test and Study Guide
Brian Williamson

Earned Benefit Program Management: Aligning, Realizing,
and Sustaining Strategy
Crispin Piney

The Entrepreneurial Project Manager
Chris Cook

Leading and Motivating Global Teams: Integrating Offshore Centers
and the Head Office
Vimal Kumar Khanna

Project and Program Turnaround
Thomas Pavelko

Project Portfolio Management in Theory and Practice: Thirty Case Studies
from around the World
Jamal Moustafaev

Project Management in Extreme Situations: Lessons from Polar Expeditions,
Military and Rescue Operations, and Wilderness Exploration
Monique Aubry and Pascal Lievre

Benefits Realization Management: Strategic Value from Portfolios,
Programs, and Projects

HCMBOK®
The Human Change Management Body of Knowledge

Third Edition

Vicente Gonçalves
Carla Campos

CRC Press
Taylor & Francis Group
Boca Raton London New York

CRC Press is an imprint of the
Taylor & Francis Group, an **informa** business
AN AUERBACH BOOK

CRC Press
Taylor & Francis Group
6000 Broken Sound Parkway NW, Suite 300
Boca Raton, FL 33487-2742

First issued in paperback 2021

© 2018 by Taylor & Francis Group, LLC
CRC Press is an imprint of Taylor & Francis Group, an Informa business

No claim to original U.S. Government works

Printed on acid-free paper

ISBN-13: 978-1-138-57647-6 (hbk)
ISBN-13: 978-1-03-209583-7 (pbk)

Visit the Taylor & Francis Web site at
http://www.taylorandfrancis.com

and the CRC Press Web site at
http://www.crcpress.com

Dedication

To my children, Yuri, Igor, and Marina, who taught me that in life everything changes, everything passes.

To my wife, an example of resilience and human behavior.

To my mother and grandmother, who taught me to persevere.

— *Vicente Gonçalves*

To my children for teaching me that love is unconditional—we just love; to my husband for his support and encouragement; to my parents and brothers for being examples that life is worth living and that we always have choices—when we cannot choose the circumstances, we can choose how we will live them. And, to all the encounters I have had throughout my life, each one of them made me a different and better person.

— *Carla Campos*

Contents

Dedication   vii

Contents   ix

Foreword by Dr. Ginger Levin   xv

Foreword by Américo Pinto   xvii

Preface   xix

Our Acknowledgments to HCMBOK®'s Collaborators   xxiii

About the Authors   xxvii

Introduction   xxix

Chapter 1: Everything Changes, Everything Passes   1

   1.1   A New Era in the Management of the Human
       Factor in Projects   1
   1.2   Is Change So Difficult?   5
   1.3   Effects of Change on the Workforce   6
   1.4   What Has Changed in the Change Processes?   8
   1.5   Change Strategies   10
       1.5.1   Imposed Changes   10
       1.5.2   Participatory Changes   11
   1.6   The Players Involved in a Change   12
   1.7   Models of Performance of Change Managers   13
   1.8   Change Management Objective   14
   1.9   Importance of the Strategic Approach to
       Change Management   16
   1.10 Project Management or Organizational Transformation? 17

Chapter 2: HCMBOK®—Human Change Management Body of Knowledge   **19**

    2.1   HCMBOK® Structure   20

Chapter 3: Project Initiation and Planning   **23**

    3.1   Define and Prepare the Sponsor of the Project   24
    3.2   Hold a Working Session to Align and Mobilize Leaders   26
    3.3   Define the Project's Purpose and Identity   29
    3.4   Mapping and Classifying Stakeholders   32
    3.5   Assess Characteristics of the Organizational Culture
         and Its Effects on the Change Efforts   36
    3.6   Define the Roles and Responsibilities of the
         Project Team   41
         3.6.1   Prepare the RACI (Responsible, Accountable,
                Consulted, and Informed) Matrix   41
         3.6.2   Define the Project Organization Chart   43
    3.7   Adjust the Physical Environment to the Project Needs   47
    3.8   Plan the Team's Assignment and Development   48
         3.8.1   Team's Assignment and Postproject
                Assignment   48
         3.8.2   Define and Implement Preliminary Training   51
    3.9   Assess the Predisposition to Changes and Their
         Impacts   52
         3.9.1   Maturity to Deal with Loss   52
         3.9.2   The Team's Level of Confidence   55
   3.10   Identify Alternatives for Knowledge Management   56
   3.11   Establish the Change Management Action Plan   57
   3.12   Plan the Project Kick-Off   60
   3.13   Develop the Change Management Strategic Plan   63
   3.14   Chapter Summary   68

Chapter 4: Acquisition   **71**

    4.1   Plan the Human Aspects of the Acquisition Process   72
    4.2   Assess Risks of Cultural Clashes between Vendors
         and the Team   73
    4.3   Define the Team's Additional Technical Training Needs   74
    4.4   Map Vendors' Leadership Styles   75

4.5   Validate Roles and Responsibilities (RACI Matrix)
        with Vendors   77
4.6   Plan Vendors' Integration into the Organizational
        Culture   77

Chapter 5: Execution   79

5.1   Carry Out the Project Kick-Off Event   79
5.2   Assess Organizational Impacts   81
5.3   Plan and Execute Learning and Acquired
        Knowledge Management   83
5.4   Feed the Project's Risk Map   86
5.5   Confirm the Stakeholders' Futures in the
        Post-Project Phase   87
5.6   Plan a Gradual Demobilization of the Project Team   90
5.7   Define Roles and Responsibilities for the
        Production Phase   91
5.8   Define Indicators to Evaluate Readiness for the Change   92

Chapter 6: Implementation   95

6.1   Assess Stakeholders' Readiness and Confidence to
        Implement the Project   96
6.2   Ensure All Leaders' Commitment to the
        Implementation   97
6.3   Hold the Implementation Decision Meeting   99
6.4   Communicate the Result of the Implementation
        Decision Meeting   101

Chapter 7: Closing   103

7.1   Execute Gradual Demobilization of the Project Team   103
7.2   Recognize Team and Individual Performances   104
7.3   Review and Document Lessons Learned   105
7.4   Ensure Preparation of Users to Train New
        Collaborators   106
7.5   Ensure Preparation of the Maintenance and Support
        Team in the Post-Project Phase   107
7.6   Ensure Adequate Reassignment of Project Members   107
7.7   Celebrate Wins and Goals Achieved   108

Chapter 8: Production (Post-Implementation)   **109**

   8.1   Ensure Change Sustainability   110

Chapter 9: Recurring Activities in All Project Phases   **115**

Chapter 10: Plan and Manage Communication   **117**

   10.1   Dimensions of Communication   118
   10.2   Elements for Consideration When Communicating   120
   10.3   Types of Project Communication   121
            10.3.1   Ordinary Communications   121
            10.3.2   Extraordinary Communications   122
   10.4   Brain Dominance Styles and Communication
            Implications   122

**Chapter 11: Create Team Spirit and Carry Out
                Reinforcement Dynamics**   **125**

Chapter 12: Encourage Participatory Processes   **129**

**Chapter 13: Manage the Environment—Conflicts,
                Motivation, Stress, and Behaviors**   **133**

   13.1   Conflict Management   133
   13.2   Motivation Management   138
   13.3   Stress Management   141
   13.4   Behavior Management   143

Chapter 14: Encourage Creativity and Innovation   **145**

   14.1   Techniques for Generating Creative Solutions   148
            14.1.1   Defining the Problem to be Solved   148
            14.1.2   Generating Ideas   149
            14.1.3   Grouping, Selection, and Enhancing   151

Chapter 15: Manage Stakeholder Engagement   **153**

Chapter 16: CMO—The Change Management Office   **165**

   16.1   Turning Strategy into Results   165
   16.2   The Concept of the CMO   166
   16.3   The Role of the CMO   168

16.4   Where to Establish the CMO   171
16.5   Examples of CMO Structures   173
16.6   Implementing a CMO is a Project and Requires
       Change Management   175

Chapter 17: Essential Competencies for Change Leaders   179

17.1   A Definition of Competency   180
17.2   Competencies for Change Leaders   180
       17.2.1   Sensitivity to Human Factors and Astuteness
                to Unveil Them; Empathic Attitude   181
       17.2.2   Capacity to Facilitate, Inspire, and Encourage
                Team Effort   181
       17.2.3   A Focus on Results, Goals, and Productivity   181
       17.2.4   Ability to Plan and Negotiate—Strategic Vision   182
       17.2.5   Ability to Manage Conflicts, Crises, and
                Opportunities   182
       17.2.6   Creativity, Inquisitiveness, Boldness, and
                Willingness to Break Paradigms   183
       17.2.7   Effectiveness as a Communicator; a Good
                Listener   183
       17.2.8   Transparency, Credibility, and Integrity   183

**Appendix I: The HCMBOK® Preliminary Approach to
                Agile Methodologies in Changes Involving
                Systems Development   185**

**Appendix II: Organizational Culture Management and
                Change Management   187**

Bibliography   191

Index   195

Foreword

While projects have been in existence since ancient times, each project, program, or portfolio has changes associated with it. These changes often are ones that add more business value for the customer and/or the sponsoring organization.

The project profession tends to focus primarily on minimizing changes in terms of scope, time, and cost and adopting an integrated change control approach. Change models, such as the 1947 one by Dr. Kurt Lewin, were among the first to focus on change as it involves people, with its emphasis on unfreezing, freezing, and refreezing. Later, in 1996, Dr. John Kotter also adopted an approach to change management in his book, *Leading Change* (Harvard Business School Press), that added to the emphasis on people.

These works and others set the stage for Vicente Gonçalves and Carla Campos's book, *The Human Change Management Body of Knowledge* (HCMBOK®). They have done an excellent job of incorporating what must be done in terms of managing people to accept the changes that result from portfolios, programs, and projects such that there then becomes a seamless integration between change and the project profession. No longer are people the forgotten but key element in ensuring that products, services, and benefits are embraced and exploited by the people who are the recipients of the outcomes. The authors further emphasize throughout the need for effective stakeholder engagement to make the entire process seamless and effective. Their HCMBOK® is a definite contribution to the profession.

Dr. Ginger Levin, PMP, PgMP, OPM3
Lighthouse Point, Florida, USA

Foreword

According to the dictionary, "Foreword" is the name given to an introductory text that briefly describes the objective of the work and provides information about its author. So, when I was invited to write this Foreword, I was immediately hit by two different feelings: I felt challenged to summarize in a few words all the contents of such a broad and meaningful work for the business world. At the same time I felt honored to be able to talk about its authors, Vicente Gonçalves and Carla Campos, whom I admire deeply for their professional and personal stories.

The great merit of this book is to address the theme of Organizational Change Management in a totally applied manner without getting lost in theoretical discussions detached from reality. Thus, the authors are able to achieve their main objective: to provide a practical guide that can be used by professionals in any field of activity.

In this book you will find a knowledge base for organizational change management consisting of processes, tools, and good practices applicable to projects of any kind.

Addressing the theme from the planning to the post-project phase, Vicente and Carla present in detail a series of recommended processes to implement and sustain organizational changes until they are properly incorporated into the company culture.

In Chapter 1 you will find concepts and introductory ideas that reinforce the strategic role of change management in organizations, and establish a new and original approach by highlighting the role of the change manager.

In Chapters 2 through 15 the authors present the HCMBOK®—Human Change Management Body of Knowledge, the heart of this work. Based on field experience, this "BOK" discusses in detail all processes related to the initiation, planning, acquisition, execution, implementation, and closing of organizational change projects. In these chapters, the authors highlight some topics that are critical to the success of projects, such as the adjustment to the culture of the organization, commitment of sponsors, engagement of stakeholders, risk management, and the fundamental measurement of the results.

In Chapter 16 you will learn about the Change Management Office (CMO), intended to support the organizational change management processes by providing skills, processes, and tools.

In the Appendixes you will find very important contributions, such as adapting the practices to agile methodologies and recommendations on the skills that are necessary to change managers for successful and organizational change management.

Vicente Gonçalves is a professional with a solid background and extensive experience—both as an executive and consultant—in different types of organizations. These years of experience have resulted in Vicente developing a rare skill—the ability to address relatively complex issues with simplicity and objectivity. Carla complements this work with her touch of a psychologist specializing in human behavior in the face of change situations.

With this work, the authors' outstanding contribution is evident not only for its content, but also because we already see the HCMBOK® being applied successfully by hundreds of professionals in several countries.

I remember very well the first time we talked, Vicente and I, about the ideas that eventually became this book. And no wonder I was one of his first supporters. In fact, it made no sense to continue treating organizational change management as a theme of minor importance. And the authors, in a pioneering way, have transformed the scenario with this book.

As Heraclitus of Ephesus once said, "The only thing that does not change is that everything changes." It is true that changes are part of the everyday life of any professional or organization, and experience has shown that underestimating them is the shortest path to failure.

Good reading and success in your projects.

Américo Pinto
Chair, PMO Global Alliance
Professor, FGV – Fundação Getúlio Vargas

Preface

Change management is a broad subject and can be applied to all different types of organizational change. The most common change drivers include: technological evolution, process reviews, crises, and consumer habit changes, as well as pressure from new business entrants, acquisitions, mergers, and organizational restructuring. They all have one characteristic in common—they affect people and their paradigms. They change the *status quo* (the way things are done) and take people out of their comfort zone.

In the first part of this book, we present the concept of change management, its players, strategies, and applicable models. In the second part we address the set of good practices, methodology, and tools that we call HCMBOK®— Human Change Management Body of Knowledge. In the third part, we introduce the concept of the *Change Management Office* (CMO) and its relation to the strategic planning of an organization. In the final parts, we list the competencies we consider to be essential to the change manager, present HCMBOK®'s preliminary approach to agile methodologies, and provide a model for managing cultural change.

We understand that, regardless of the driver, a change must be planned and implemented as a project.

Imagine that you want to move to a new home. Even if you do not realize it, you will be developing a project. The widespread definition of a project is a set of activities developed for a particular purpose, with a beginning and an end and a predefined budget.

In the new home example, you will need to plan how much you can spend, whether renting a unit or buying a property. You will have to decide, based on some criteria, where you want to live and details such as number of rooms, parking space, bathrooms, if a multi-unit dwelling allows dogs and cats, etc.

You will also need to involve and engage stakeholders, particularly challenging if you have children in their teens. Their sense of loss can be immense because change may lead to the disruption of personal ties with friends from the school, neighborhood, and current home. If the change is to another city or country, the project becomes even more complex because there are many factors that can influence the engagement. While some may perceive the change as positive, others may experience a tremendous discomfort, resisting the change and using all their strength to keep the situation as it is.

Then you will reach the implementation of the project, when you will have to sign contracts, handle all the paperwork, approve dwelling modifications, and, finally, pack and transfer your assets to the new home.

At this point, if you do not have a good execution plan, your life may become a disaster. For months you will suffer the pressure from other stakeholders, especially those not engaged in the change, and the impact of adapting to the new environment, which will require precious time looking for things that are no longer where they used to be.

During the implementation, surprises will occur. Where can you find a bakery with products as good as those you used to find a block away from your previous home? What is the best route to work? Who are your neighbors? Who can you trust or just ask for a favor? All this is part of the natural adaptation to the new, the unknown, which surely will bring some sense of loss. However, if the project has been well planned and implemented, many gains from the change will also be quickly perceived and valued.

Some stakeholders will suffer more than others. Each human being has his or her pace for adapting to change, and this will demand sustaining the change until it has been fully consolidated. In the case of teenage children, they will make new friends, will eventually adapt to the new school and to the benefits of the new home—for example, having a larger room with more privacy.

However, in some cases, this adaptation may take longer or will never even take place.

In this hypothetical example, we are assuming that you want to move, that is, the commitment to change is a natural and expected fact. Now, assume that this option does not exist, that for some reason you had to move. In this case, the pain deriving from the change will probably be more intensely perceived by the entire family, and the impact may be significant enough to warrant more changes in the future.

Managing a move to a new home is a project that can be simple or complex, depending on the circumstances and budget available. However, if the stakeholders are not involved and engaged, the move will surely be much more traumatic.

I remember that some years ago a good friend of mine received a great work proposal that would require moving from São Paulo to Rio de Janeiro.

Although living in Rio de Janeiro is the dream of many people, his teenage children were frustrated about having to change schools and leave their friends. His wife had to leave her job and look for another one in a city, which although less than 320 miles away, has totally different characteristics.

The impact from the change was such that even with the compensation of a great career opportunity, one year later pressure from the stakeholders turned the dream into a nightmare, the solution to which was abandoning the original project and returning to their city of origin.

After all, what went wrong? The job was great, the city offered good leisure options. In the popular imagination, many Brazilians would like to live in Rio de Janeiro, but the move project did not achieve its goals.

Many motivators can explain the return of this family to their original comfort zone, but certainly the influence of the stakeholders was one of the determinants for the project not working as planned.

The HCMBOK® Model

We believe that, before the changes are consolidated in the organization, they need to touch the human being. That is why we call our body of knowledge the Human Change Management Body of Knowledge. We believe that it is through human change that we achieve organizational change.

The principles and practices contained herein can be applied to any type of change. For didactic reasons, the HCMBOK® was conceived by relating the change management activities to the steps traditionally followed in project management. The application of the HCMBOK® should be adapted to the nature and characteristics of each project. For example, a project that does not include external vendors can disregard the activities planned for them and follow only the relevant ones.

Our main objective with this edition of the HCMBOK® is to provide readers with a reference for managing the essential activities in change projects with specific emphasis on the impacts of the human factor, without claiming to be exhaustive.

Managing change means humanizing it. It means to design the project from the standpoint of the people involved in order to avoid the fact that natural resistance has an impact on planned objectives.

The change manager's creativity and sensitivity are the primary components that cannot be replaced by any methodology, framework, or body of knowledge.

A project, even if it uses a very well structured change management methodological approach, if conducted mechanically, still can run a serious risk of facing resistance and failing. However, a project managed intuitively by someone who takes into account human complexity and takes a position that shows empathy for the main stakeholders affected by the change can be very successful.

Of course, the ideal situation is the combination of talent to manage human issues, and the technique provided by a good guide to the methodology, best practices, and tools. If, in addition, this change manager has the set of core competencies of a change leader, extraordinary results will be achieved through the engagement of the involved stakeholders.

Our Acknowledgments to HCMBOK®'s Collaborators

The Human Change Management Body of Knowledge (HCMBOK®) is a work in progress and will continue to evolve. After all, everything changes all the time, and so we have to adapt continuously.

The continuous evolution of HCMBOK® is the result of a joint effort of several people who send us suggestions, criticisms, and comments based on their experiences.

Without this cooperative effort, HCMBOK® would be restricted to our studies and experiences. Our most sincere thanks to the collaborators who, by sharing their experiences, ideas, and tools, make HCMBOK® a richer and more complete, global, multicultural guide.

There follows, in alphabetical order, a list of the collaborators who have supported the development of the HCMBOK® by improving the description of good practices, proofreading, and inclusion of new activities and macro-activities:

Angel Gabriel Olivo Diaz – HCMBOK – Argentina

Arnaldo Di Petta – HCMP – Brazil

Carlos Eduardo Bagatin – HCMMP – Brazil

José Aromando – HCMP – Argentina

Paulina Orozco – HCMP – Ecuador

Paula Link – HCMBOK – Australia

Renata Casado – HCMP – Australia

Rodrigo Alejandro Franco Carillo – HCMMP – Colombia

Sandra L. Gusmán – HCMMP – Colombia

Stacey Leslie – HCMP – South Africa

Tatiana Dale – HCMP – Brazil

Wilson Casado – HCMP – Australia

Amanda Palazón – HCMP – Spain

For definition of macro-activity 3.2: Hold a working session to align and mobilize leaders

Cristiane Gazel Trindade – HCMP – Brazil

For definition of macro-activity 5.8: Define indicators to evaluate readiness for the change

Edgar Alvarez – HCMP – Ecuador

For collaboration on

Appendix I: The HCMBOK® Preliminary Approach to Agile Methodologies in Changes Involving Systems Development

Appendix II: Organizational Culture Management and Change Management

For developing: The conceptual model for organizational culture management (Figure AII.2)

Gustavo Acha – HCMP – Argentina

For contribution to the development of the Change Management Strategic Plan

Special Acknowledgments

Callie Gargiulo McDowell

The Third Edition of HCMBOK® would not have been possible without the collaboration of Callie Gargiulo McDowell, Principal, CGM Consulting. Callie's contribution was not only in terms of text revision but also enriching the content with her extensive experience in project and change management.

To Callie, our eternal gratefulness and appreciation for the amazing result of your work!

Ginger Levin

For her patience supporting us to make this book more complete and accurate. Her generosity in sharing knowledge certainly added value to the final result of this book.

John Wyzalek and Taylor & Francis Group

For their belief in this book project as well as their support in making it the best it can be.

Lynne Lackenbach, Marje Pollack, Susan Culligan, and Theron Shreve – DerryField Publishing Services

For teaching me that any book is a result of team work. For sure, their tireless support and meticulous work made this book more precise and easier to read.

About the Authors

Carla Campos

Psychologist with postgraduate studies in People Management; Assessment Consultant; Certified Professional and Personal Coach with International Certification from ECA (European Coaching Association) and GCC (Global Coaching Community); postgraduate studies in Human Resources Management from AVM–UCAM and in Cognitive-Behavioral Therapy from CPAF; member of the Brazilian Association of Cognitive Psychotherapy (ABPC) and the Association of Cognitive Therapies of Rio de Janeiro (ATCRIO); and co-author of the book *Tanatologia–Temas Impertinentes.*

In recent years, Carla has dedicated herself to the study of human development, change management, people management, coaching, outplacement, talent recruitment and selection, losses, and resilience. She is the Vice President of the Human Change Management Institute and is a frequent lecturer and workshop facilitator as well as a consultant.

Contact: carla@hucmi.com

Vicente Gonçalves

His education includes performance arts, social sciences, and information technology. He holds a postgraduate degree in Marketing and an MBA degree from COPPEAD–UFRJ. He enhanced his management and leadership knowledge at MIT Sloan Executive Education, Boston, USA, IMD–Lausanne, Switzerland, and AMANA-KEY. Complementing his diverse profile, Vicente is an actor, author, director, drama teacher, poet, and writer. During recent years, he has published several articles on creativity, innovation, and change management.

For 28 years he was a consultant and executive in national and global companies, having received 12 innovation-, project-, and change-management–related awards from renowned publications. He was elected CIO (Chief Information Officer) of the Year in the media and communication area four times. In 2010 he received the Assis Chateaubriand commendation from the São Paulo Arts and Literature Academy for relevant services in the area of scientific and human development. He is a guest professor and lecturer in several organizations, including PMI, PMO Alliance, CIO Summit, PMO Master Class, among others.

In addition to being CEO of the Human Change Management Institute, Vicente is a consultant in the areas of creativity and innovation, change management, conflict management, team creation, and integration. His extensive experience includes work in Brazil, Argentina, Australia, Canada, Chile, Colombia, Ecuador, India, Mexico, Peru, Spain, South Africa, the United States, and Uruguay.

Contact: vicente@hucmi.com

Additional information about the Human Change Management Institute is available at www.hucmi.com.

Introduction

We often hear of projects that ended with some unmet expectation in terms of deadline, cost, or quality. In fact, we have rarely found projects that did not face any difficulty in relation to at least one of these variables, if not all of them. This is not a specific feature of information technology (IT) projects but of all types of ventures, despite the huge advances provided by project management methodologies in recent decades.

After all, what makes only 57% of projects finish within their initial budgets and 51% within their initial schedule, according to the *Pulse of the Profession®* (PMI, 2017)?

We believe there are various causes, but a characteristic common to all project management methodologies is the little attention paid to a major component— change management, or, in other words, the focus on the human being and its uniqueness.

According to a study carried out by PM SURVEY.ORG in 2013 (a global initiative of PMI® chapters), 75% of the cases of failure in the implementation of Project Management Offices (PMOs) in organizations with revenues over $1 billion are related to cultural resistance and issues that were not properly addressed. This rate varies from 76% to 60% in companies with revenues up to $100 million. Lack of sponsorship is another important factor mentioned by 75% of the large organizations as the cause of failure in this same type of endeavor. Still according to this benchmark, in the list of problems that occurred more frequently in project management in organizations with revenues between $500 million and $1 billion, communication is number one, mentioned in 86% of the cases. It is noteworthy that the survey data in PMSURVEY.ORG also showed deficiencies related directly to organizational change management.

Another important source of information is the study, *Enabling Organizational Change through Strategic Initiatives* (PMI, 2014a), which shows that only 18% of organizations report being highly effective at organizational change management. This same source mentions that organizations that combine standardized project and program management practices and an effective change management, if compared with those that do not use the same approach, increase their success rate to meet the goals of strategic initiatives by more than 100%. Their rate of completing the strategic initiatives on schedule and on budget is on average 80% better.

Therefore, we believe that a solid change management approach is critical for the success of a project, no matter its type.

There is no magic formula to manage change. Each project is unique because it affects a different culture and, most important, different people, at different moments in time.

The world is not static, and organizations are also experiencing constant changes. As Heraclitus of Ephesus, a pre-Socratic philosopher, stated: "No man ever steps in the same river twice."

However, following a methodology, using good practices and adequate tools to manage the change process can largely reduce project risks.

It is not by chance that the Fifth Edition of the *PMBOK® Guide*, launched in 2013, contains a new area of knowledge—Stakeholder Management—thus showing a clear concern about the relevance of human factors for successful project management (PMI, 2013a).

No methodology will replace the change manager's sensitivity, whether he or she is a professional dedicated to this activity or a project manager holding several roles.

Following a script with steps and activities recognized as good change management practice is a huge step forward to ensure the success of a project. And this is what HCMBOK® addresses—an effective way to deal with human issues. It is not the only way, but no way can work without the human sensitivity of leaders to manage the human factor before the challenge of breaking old paradigms and changing the *status quo*.

Chapter 1

Everything Changes, Everything Passes

1.1. A New Era in the Management of the Human Factor in Projects

The Human Factor in Project Leadership in the Third Millennium

Knowledge of project management has evolved a lot over the past 30 years, but only recently has it started to consider management of the human factor as a key area of expertise for professionals involved in project management.

In the past, good project managers were those who achieved their goals within the expected timeframe and cost parameters, with the quality and scope defined at the outset. Today, executive management and shareholders expect them to go further, requiring that projects deliver the strategic objectives that motivated the undertaking, that is, what the organization expected would change after the project.

This challenge includes an even more complex and unpredictable component than processes, hardware, or software—the human being. No matter how good the product or service delivered as a result of a project is, it will only bring value to the organization if people use it properly.

Since the beginning of this decade, a movement has been growing to make management of the human factor popular among project, process, and human resources professionals as well as leaders in all areas.

1

If, in the past, this was a discipline for experts, academics, and psychologists only, today the third generation of organizational change management has turned managing the human factor into a key competence for professionals of the third millennium.

Over the past decades, the pressure for organizations to remain competitive and profitable has led to the development of new tactics, such as process redesign, implementation of technological components, restructuring, and mergers and acquisitions, among many other projects that required a strong adaptation of the human component to the organizational environment.

The promises that justified huge investments in management models based on technologies of the information age, such as enterprise resource planning (ERP), customer relationship management (CRM), and business intelligence (BI), among others, have generated expectations that were not always met, leaving a legacy of frustration in many organizations. Despite the massive capital investments, shareholders and top managers realized that the success of the projects depended greatly on people to achieve their business goals.

In the 1940s, Kurt Lewin put forth the first theories about human behavior during change processes. Lewin, considered by many thought leaders to be the father of social psychology, inspired a host of thinkers in the 1980s and 1990s who shaped the *first generation* that established the structure of the discipline we know today as organizational change management.

Until the middle of the 1990s, change management was rarely applied in projects. It was limited to a small group of companies in the forefront of human factor management that used the knowledge of experts to support Human Resources.

Moving against the psychological line, the so-called Big Five, the five largest global consulting firms, developed an operational change management approach, which almost always focused on organizational impacts, training, and communication, applied especially in the implementation of ERP projects.

The next wave of change saw the emergence of frameworks being adopted as standards for some companies—the major milestone of the *second generation* of organizational change management.

Even today, these approaches, which originated from academic models or highly specialized consulting firms, are inspiring references that are often used by change management experts. However, they are seldom well understood and do not adequately sensitize technical executives and project managers. It is very difficult for the logical, Cartesian, and quantitative thinking of exact science professionals to translate into practical project activities proposals such as "create a sense of urgency."

At the turn of the millennium, a large number of professionals from these consulting firms created small companies that helped consolidate change management as a crucial practice, especially in strategic or large projects.

However, the world went on changing, and so did change management. Failures in large change projects, especially in the technological world, kept piling up, while those responsible for project management offices (PMOs) and project managers realized that, without people, projects can meet their deadlines and achieve their cost, scope, and quality goals, but they do not always achieve the strategic objectives that motivated the investment.

Beginning early in the 21st century, the spread of the practice of managing organizational changes by global consulting firms attracted the attention of experts in the area. They began to organize into professional associations with the objective of developing standards, processes, and a code of ethics for change managers. Thus began the *third generation* of organizational change management—a well-organized structure initiated by the major consulting firms, which contributed a significant amount of professional knowledge.

In 2012, change management took on a new character in the translation of the hermetic language of experts and academic masters into the practical and objective world of project managers with the creation of the Human Change Management Institute (HUCMI®) and its base of knowledge, *The Human Change Management Body of Knowledge* (HCMBOK®).

Parallel to the movements promoted by other associations of experts, the Project Management Institute (PMI) published the Fifth Edition of *A Guide to the Project Management Body of Knowledge* (*PMBOK® Guide*) in 2013, bringing as its big news a new area of knowledge little addressed until then among project managers: *stakeholder management* (PMI, 2013a).

A few months later, the PMI confirmed its focus on the human issue by launching *Managing Change in Organizations: A Practice Guide* (PMI, 2013b), with fundamentals that suggested that organizational change management would be more and more present in *PMBOK® Guide*.

It is this growing popularization of human factor management in projects, spread mainly by the Association of Change Management Professionals® (ACMP®), PMI, and HUCMI®, that typifies the *third generation* of organizational change management. The discipline went from the "what to do" phase to the "how to do it" phase in terms of the universe of project management.

Change management was never seen as important a discipline as it is today. Data from the *Pulse of the Profession®*, a 2017 report organized by the PMI, shows that 67% of senior executives consider the creation of a culture receptive to organizational change as very high or somewhat high priority (PMI, 2017).

The project management discipline has evolved significantly over the past three decades, but only recently has it begun to see management of the human factor as an essential area of knowledge that cannot be restricted to organizational change management professionals.

The organizational change management expert will always exist—a professional with extensive experience, knowledge, and skills to address the most complex aspects of the subject. However, the Human Resources (HR) professionals, project, program, and portfolio managers of the future have already realized that they must have a good command of human factor management in order to continuously increase rates of success in achieving the strategic objectives that drive organizations.

After all, there are no projects without people, nor are there organizational changes that should not be structured as projects.

When we speak of a new generation in the technological world, we are almost always speaking of substitute technologies, a new generation of technologies that overlaps the earlier generation, which is then doomed to disappear. When it comes to human issues, however, the dynamic is different. Generations are added and inspire one another, but do not substitute for an earlier generation. Rather they are directed to new audiences, with similar fundamentals but a new approach. In this particular case, third-generation (3G) change management is a translation of the concepts of prior generations for a universe of professionals who demand a more practical and objective language targeting their reality, enhanced by some new knowledge and more connected with the contemporary world of project management.

This is the approach of HCMBOK®, already used in more than 27 countries. According to this approach, the human factor is an integral part of the strategy for any kind of project. Twenty-five out of HCMBOK®'s 48 macro-activities are carried out before the execution phase is started, thus fine-tuning from the planning phase how to communicate the project, choose the sponsors who can best influence the success of the venture, and define the purpose that can best connect stakeholders with specific changes and strategies to reduce resistance and expand human engagement.

In its approach, HCMBOK® organizes a sequence of macro-activity techniques to manage cultural and human behavior issues in a structured way, while providing an arsenal of skills that are essential to project managers—for example, participatory process, conflict, motivation and behavior management, creation of team spirit, empathetic communication, creativity, and innovation.

In short, the *HCMBOK® Guide* was developed to facilitate integration into any methodology. It addresses human factor–related *issues in the language of project managers* and complements the stakeholder management approach developed by the PMI.

So, be prepared. Delivering a project within the planned deadline, cost, quality, and scope is no longer enough. The expectation now is that the strategic objectives that motivated the project are measured by qualitative and quantitative goals, which require engagement of the human component to be achieved.

No matter the title that prevails—Organizational Change Management or Stakeholder Management—it is clear that the third generation of human factor management in projects (3G CM) is here to stay and has become an essential discipline for project managers of the third millennium.

1.2. Is Change So Difficult?

Looking at the anthropological context, the human being was shaped over millennia not to change but to maintain the status quo whenever possible. This was the case when the first hunter-gatherer societies were established. People were nomads, forced to move from one geographic location to another, whenever the hunting or gathering area was depleted or became unworkable for any other reason. This change involved a number of risks: the risk of not finding another area in time that would ensure their survival; and, worst of all, the risk of finding this other area already occupied by another group. Encountering another group would most likely lead to violence and other unpredictable consequences.

Centuries later, people began to practice agriculture and cattle raising, and no longer depended on hunting and gathering to survive. Societies could then settle down without the need for constant geographic moves. The first villages were established, and soon their protection strategies, such as walls and barriers, reduced the need for moving. Over the millennia, these walls became taller and stronger and whenever someone had to go outside that safe zone—to the forests and fields—the sensation of risk and discomfort was present.

Modern society, in the anthropological context, has maintained this instinct of aversion to change given the inherent risk that change represents to the collective unconsciousness. The now psychological "walls" and "barriers" are still alive in every human being. As Charles Darwin stated, "Man still carries in his physical structure the indelible mark of his primitive ancestors."

Not by chance, Heraclitus of Ephesus realized that "Nothing but change is permanent." Later, Charles Darwin endorsed this same theory in his study, *The Origin of Species,* which addresses "natural selection." Darwin verified that species are constantly changing and that "It is not the strongest of the species nor the most intelligent that survives. It is the one that is most adaptable to change." In the area of change management in today's world, no statement is more relevant.

Human behavior varies over time, although it presents stable macro-characteristics. In our view, in the contemporary world the influence of more superficial social relations on the Y generation (also known as millennials) and the Z generation has implications for values and behaviors. The intense and frequent changes promoted by technological revolution are present in the daily lives of young people. This scenario is likely to have effects on the adaptability of these generations, making attachment to the status quo less relevant to their lives. The negative side of these generations' attitude toward change is their lack of sensitivity to the conservatism of the previous generations. Sometimes they create an impression of disregard, and make more simultaneous changes than the organization can support.

Only time will tell how the deep changes that society is experiencing will influence human behavior. Even so, the challenge of promoting an organizational change continues to be a difficult and complex task, which must be driven through people to achieve a higher rate of success.

1.3. Effects of Change on the Workforce

Human beings change spontaneously when the discomfort of being in a certain situation seems greater than the change. However, some changes can be very difficult for humans to process, and put us in a state of mourning.

Grief is a necessary state of transition for people to process the losses, experience feelings such as anxiety, immobilization, denial, fear, anger, bargaining, guilt, depression, and finally, work on the resignification of, and stabilization in, a new adapted state.

When we know in advance that we will experience a change that will be perceived as a loss, we go into a state of anticipatory grief. This is a common phenomenon in human behavior when we feel a major change we can experience in life—death of a loved one or our own—is imminent. This was first described by doctors who noted that the wives of soldiers sent to war went into a state of mourning even before their death was confirmed.

Within hospital psychology, anticipatory grief, if properly dealt with, can be positive for people to process impending losses, preparing patients and their families for an irreversible situation. Patients are able to do things they would like to have done but had not had a chance to do. Friends and family can resolve outstanding conflicts, thus minimizing the effect of guilt in the mourning phase that follows the fatal outcome.

Anticipatory grief can also be found in many organizations when a change is about to happen. If the change has not been adequately communicated or understood, its effect will be negative, creating a feeling of anxiety and fear fueled by uncertainty about the future.

Often this change does not even exist. It is the result of a myth or an organizational environment of low trust in the leaders and organization. The effects of organizational anticipatory grief, in this case, are very serious. People come to a standstill, becoming angry and even aggressive. Surviving, maintaining the status quo, is more important than anything else. Productivity is affected. Creativity gives way to stagnation. Corridors and common areas such as cafeterias and break rooms become information points. Truths are created or distorted, creating an atmosphere of pessimism toward the future. Knowledge is no longer shared by the workforce and is now used as a strategy in an alleged dispute over the maintenance of personal positions in the organizational structure. When the change occurs, resistance has already been magnified by the general state of early suffering promoted by lack of timely communication or even inadequate initial communication of the changes that were to come.

Figure 1.1 compares human relations at the personal and professional levels. In this case, the behavior at the professional level reflects a situation where changes were not managed or where changes and their results were managed ineffectively.

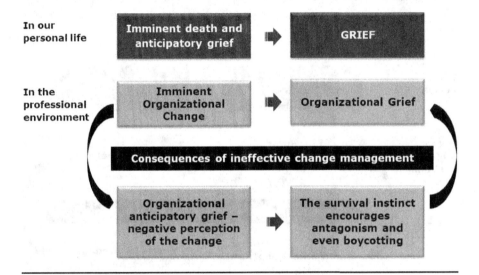

Figure 1.1   Consequences of ineffective change management.

Many of the HCMBOK® activities that we will present in this Guide are designed to prevent people from going into the organizational anticipatory grief state due to a negative perception of the change. These activities, when performed properly and in a timely manner, generate psychological security, reduce negative impacts on the organizational climate, minimize resistance or antagonism, and increase resilience, thus preparing the organization to better accept the change. Note that resilience is not impermeability. Resilience means being affected by the change, but having the ability to adapt and go back to a defined state after adjusting to a new reality.

When the organizational anticipatory grief is well managed, as in hospital psychology, many actions can be implemented to channel negative perceptions of change to a more positive situation through better opportunities for processing losses and adjusting behaviors as necessary to adapt to the future situation. We thus leave a situation where what we feel (uncontrollable instance) is dominant and gradually replace what we feel with how we act, how we manage our attitudes before the change (controllable instance).

Even when we cannot choose the circumstances we will experience, we can always choose *how* we will experience them.

Understanding the need for an organizational change does not necessarily eliminate the pain that the change will cause, but for many it makes the situation more transparent, gives meaning to things, eliminates distorted perceptions of reality, and accelerates the process of adjustment to the future state of the organization. Figure 1.2 again compares the changes at the personal and professional levels. This time the comparison reflects the deployment of effective change management.

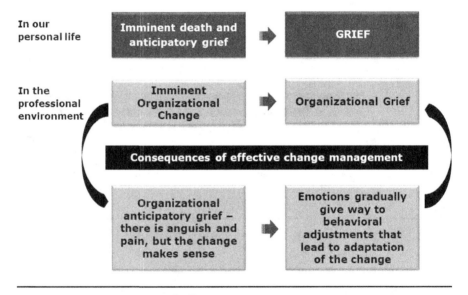

Figure 1.2   Consequences of effective change management.

1.4. What Has Changed in the Change Processes?

The world has always been changing and human beings, with greater or lesser pain, have always adapted in order to survive. What we have seen over recent decades is a great acceleration in the speed with which changes take place. While it took the telephone 76 years to reach 50 million users, the cell phone achieved this milestone in just 5 years, and Facebook in 2 years.

Facebook, which until 2004 was a social network oriented only to some universities, was opened to the public in 2006, and in 2017 it already had 2 billion users. If Facebook were a country, it would have the largest population in the world. Orkut and Myspace were great stars up until 2009, but they have already been abandoned by practically all of their users.

WhatsApp, which launched in 2010, emerged with tremendous speed: In 2017, WhatsApp reached 1 billion people around the world. It will probably have as many users as Facebook within a few years.

Within those same few years, a reader of this book will probably have migrated from Facebook to a new type of relationship through social networks still unknown to us.

What changes with this introduction of new technology is not only its use in an almost omnipresent way, but also people's habits and behaviors—the way relationships are created and deconstructed. According to research carried out by the American Academy of Matrimonial Lawyers in 2011, Facebook is cited in one out of every five divorces in the United States.

2011 saw the start of the so-called Arab Spring movement, which toppled dictators in Muslim-majority countries. The Arab Spring was possible only thanks to new communication alternatives that mobilized thousands of people, despite state control over traditional media. Since 2014, terrorist movements have incorporated the use of social networks as a strategy to recruit new members worldwide and reveal their atrocities to shock and intimidate their enemies.

In business, all changes in social and marketing behavior require organizational adjustments. The competitive setting is no longer the same. Former differentiators are disappearing and being replaced by new strategies that are more appropriate for the demands of the new generations, who have also deconstructed traditional concepts of brand valuation and loyalty.

Who would have dared to say that in 2016 the largest taxi service in the world would be Uber, which does not own one single car?

Internally, organizations have replaced repetitive productivity (a phenomenon in which work is measured by parameters based exclusively on volume produced), with creative productivity (a phenomenon in which work is measured by a person's, or team's, capacity to continuously seek improvement and advancement in the way business processes are carried out).

Old people- and organizational-climate-management processes that worked effectively for decades are becoming obsolete. Old motivating factors do not have the same effect on new generations. The old dream of spending years or even one's entire career in the same organization is outdated. The boundary between professional and personal life has blurred. The challenges in managing people and teams are immense and will require adjustments in the current paradigms so that organizations can maintain desired levels of productivity.

Everything changes, everything passes, but what we can see right now is that organizations will have to reinvent themselves to address the challenges of a world that has changed exponentially. The technological revolution is still in its infancy. Much, much more will come, directly influencing the behavior of people and the way they consume products and services. Organizations will undergo more and more restructuring of their processes; the way they conduct their business will also be reviewed and revised several times.

The way work is organized is already undergoing deep transformation in countries such as France and Germany, where a large number of professionals, in particular migrants from Eastern Europe, prefer to work autonomously or as micro-entrepreneurs in a legal state of informality. This factor alone has caused the total number of participants in the government's social security program to plunge by more than 25% in the past 10 years.

In this setting, there will only be space for the most adaptable organizations. Companies, even those that rely mostly on technology, are essentially made up of people; changes *will* impact this workforce. The success of their evolution, and in some cases, revolution, depends heavily on the ability of organizations to manage the human factor in their change projects—the only way companies will be able to retain their most valuable asset, human beings—engaged, forming high-performance teams.

We are living a moment in human history when what is changing is the speed with which change takes place.

And what else is coming? Change—the only certainty.

1.5. Change Strategies

1.5.1. Imposed Changes

There are changes that are unavoidable; the only option is to adapt or die. These are *imposed changes*, which do not allow for negotiation or planned management.

An earthquake that destroys an entire city or the sudden bankruptcy of a company are examples of changes that cannot be managed by a central player. They are imposed, and self-managing of change is the only option for the parties involved.

Many companies use the imposed approach as a management strategy. They are mainly hierarchy-based companies where, to quote an old proverb, "When drums beat, laws are silent."

The following is not an unusual comment about change management: "My company has an owner. He orders and that is it. There is no such thing as change management. Those who do not adapt are fired." In fact, imposed changes do not require management, nor do they create engagement opportunities. They often take place by coercion.

The effect of imposed changes on the organization's atmosphere and productivity is harmful. *Presenteeism*, a phenomenon where the company's workforce is present but not engaged with the organization's objectives, is ubiquitous. The bodies are there but the souls are elsewhere.

People treated like beings incapable of contributing to the organization's evolution respond with *repetitive productivity*, that is, production that can be measured so that individual goals are achieved.

The imposed culture is marked by individualism. Teams are unnecessary because superior beings are the only ones capable of making correct decisions. Treated as people incapable of creativity and unable to contribute to the organization's evolution, they accept this passive state as lesser beings and begin to perform as assets with an expiration date and minimal loyalty. To achieve the state of supreme beings, internal competition borders on disloyalty. People feel like disposable objects. This is the "objectification of people," a phenomenon described by Dr. Paulo Gaudêncio in the book, *Men at Work* (1999).

1.5.2. Participatory Changes

Participatory changes are those that, having an objective as a starting point, are concerned about creating purpose, promoting engagement, and giving a broader sense to the required transition. These changes take into account the human factor and its complexity.

This approach, although harder to implement, adds more value to the organization. The culture is that of creative productivity, the one capable of improving procedures and exceeding goals, innovating and continuously renewing the organization.

Team spirit occurs more easily, almost spontaneously, as everyone feels part of an integrated system, working toward the same objective. The feeling of belonging is common to everyone; the pride of being part of the organization involves even the individuals' families and closest friends.

Often, even outside working hours, the team is connected and comes up with ideas to improve processes and promote organizational growth. People treated with dignity respond with loyalty and engagement.

Following is a brief story that illustrates this phenomenon:

> *A passer-by meets two carpenters cutting wood for construction. One wears a frown on his face. He saws the wood without bothering to make the best use of the wood or the barbs, and stacks the cut pieces carelessly. The other*

shows purpose and hums while he chooses the best slats to saw. He carefully removes the barbs and stacks each cut piece in the sequence they will be used in the next phase of the process. The curious passer-by notices the situation, approaches the carpenters, and asks the first:

"What are you doing?"

The man answers harshly:

"Cutting wood, can't you see?"

The passer-by then approaches the second carpenter and asks the same question. He answers smiling:

"I am building a school."

Because change is ever present and necessary for organizations to stay competitive, the way change is handled will also have a profound effect on shaping its culture. Therefore it is worth reflecting on questions such as:

- ❑ Which one of the two carpenters will promote greater collective production? The repetitive one, not engaged with the objective, or the creative one, committed to the result as a whole?
- ❑ Which change strategy will be able to yield better results within the planned time frame?
- ❑ Which change strategy will contribute to the organization's growth, and which one will strengthen the culture, capable of taking the organization to a higher level of competitiveness?

1.6. The Players Involved in a Change

The players involved in a change initiative are called *stakeholders*. A stakeholder is an entity, an individual or a group of individuals that will be directly or indirectly affected by the change. A stakeholder can be any company employee, a vendor, a union, customers, governmental bodies, etc.

Identifying and classifying these stakeholders is fundamental for the development of a change management strategy. This subject will be explored in detail in Chapter 3, covering the planning phase of the project. As the term *stakeholder* will appear repeatedly going forward, we thought it better to define the term at the beginning of the book for easier understanding.

In a simplified view, stakeholders most commonly position themselves in two ways, as indicated in Figure 1.3.

Figure 1.3 Most common positioning of stakeholders.

1.7. Models of Performance of Change Managers

Change management is no longer a subject exclusive to experts. In the contemporary world, every professional who promotes organizational change needs to have at least minimal knowledge about it.

Throughout HCMBOK®, we will use the term *change manager* when addressing the human factor aspects of a role that a range of individuals may play during a project, as explained in the paragraphs that follow.

In small projects, when the project manager acts practically alone, managing time, cost, quality, scope, etc., he or she will have to manage the human factor as well. The same goes for small changes carried out by process improvement (PI) and human resources (HR) professionals and leaders in any area where a change is necessary.

As for substantial changes, the project manager will have a support team consisting of professionals specialized in the different areas of the project, including organizational change management.

Even so, this project manager needs to have a minimal understanding of the principles of human factor management in change processes so that he or she can interact with the team responsible for this area and act as an agent of change—developing strategies to manage stakeholders' engagement, conflicts, stress, behaviors, motivation, participatory processes, and empathic communication, as well as encouraging creativity and innovation.

In short, whether the leader of a change manages all aspects of a project alone or with the support of a specialized team dedicated exclusively to human issues, mastering organizational change management is an essential skill that will be part of the educational background of successful professionals of today and in the future.

Any and all change should be organized as a project, just as any and all projects will generate changes. The change management activities are intrinsically linked to project management and vice versa. Thus, the best practice is to merge the change management or human factor activities and the other activities of the project into a single work plan, a single approach.

The same way a project schedule includes activities related to risk management, quality, acquisition, integration, etc., change management activities, which have a deadline for completion and generate end products, must be part of the common project management tool used for planning.

Managing change as an activity separate from the project is a mistake that we still find with some frequency, but one that should be avoided.

By including change management in an organization's project management methodology and good practices, it will eventually become part of the organizational culture and will be practiced not only by those on the project team, but also by company leadership, including executives, sponsors, and co-sponsors of the project.

With time, all projects will include human factor management. This approach has been beneficial in organizations that have recognized that promoting a culture of continuous organizational transformation is more important than just completing a project within the planned schedule, cost, and quality.

1.8. Change Management Objective

According to its classic definition, change management is taking a person or organization from a current state to a desired state. However, in the view of HCMBOK®, the objective of the discipline we call *change management* is to plan, apply, measure and monitor *human factor management* actions in a change project, increasing the chances of achieving or exceeding expected results. We see no conflict between the objective that we defined for change management and its classic definition. In fact, we see convergence, because expanding the chances of achieving the expected results means bringing an organization to its desired future state.

We do not want to lose sight of the concept of corporate environment humanization. After all, there are no companies without people. We believe that widespread adoption of change management in organizations will be possible when we make it more tangible and understandable to top management. Therefore, HCMBOK® has adopted a pragmatic objective for change management, which deals with what we believe to be of interest to organizations in the language of the executives who lead the business. In short, for the top management and shareholders, change management should be a discipline to help them achieve the strategic goals of the organization.

Any change brings some discomfort to the people affected. However, change is inevitable for the evolution of organizations. Those companies that do not change do not evolve; they may become obsolete and ultimately may end in failure. This will affect all internal and external stakeholders, either directly or indirectly.

Change management is essentially the act of moving from a current state, through a transition, into a future design state. During this transition there is often a reduction in productivity, and readjustment is required. Figure 1.4 represents this transition phase, known as the "valley of despair."

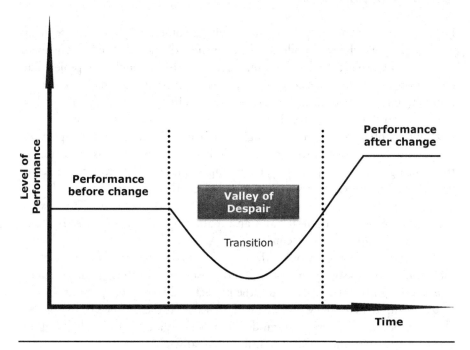

Figure 1.4   The Valley of Despair.

This transition phase is inevitable, but it can be managed, and its time span and impacts can be significantly reduced. No one changes without going through the valley, but those who camp in it suffer more. Change management is the guide that promotes the strategy and actions capable of taking those involved in the change through this valley as quickly as possible.

Change management is not an operating activity, but rather a strategic activity, and it must be part of the project from the time of its initial planning phase. In organizations with a high level of maturity in this area, change management is applied right from the development of the organizational strategic plan, as we will show in Chapter 16.

Our change management approach is focused on the human factor in a holistic way. We take into account not only the collective issues but also the individual aspects, as every person is unique and irreplaceable. Individuals' activities can be replaced, but their knowledge, skills, story, and life experience are their own, just like their DNA. It is by raising awareness, engaging or even persuading the human being, that we will achieve the intended organizational changes.

1.9. Importance of the Strategic Approach to Change Management

During a recent consulting engagement with a company in a market segment with high potential for pollution, we evaluated the change management approach of a project designed to outsource the printing pool. The project had been conceived as part of a strategic objective to improve cost management. Its initial design was focused exclusively on outsourcing printing functions by hiring a company that specializes in this type of process and technology.

Printers, often dedicated to a single user, would be gathered into "printing pools" and a printing control system would be implemented, thus rationalizing the printing activities. Apparently, a low-impact project. However, a more careful look at the stakeholders' evaluation showed that the project would meet strong resistance from the users who, for as long as the company had existed, had exclusive printers right at hand and managed their printing needs themselves, without any corporate control.

Certainly, this project would affect a comfort zone that would turn excellent intentions into a reason for complaints and resistance. The strength of the antagonists was significant enough to put the project and its original goals at risk.

Assessing the corporate context, it was clear that the purpose of the project also included another strategic guideline of the organization—cultivating an image of an environmentally responsible company.

Without losing focus on the planned benefits of cost reduction, the purpose of the project expanded to include the concept of a "green company," committed to managing the printing volume and reducing the costs and environmental impact—a purpose that could mobilize the entire organization. The Environment Department, which had not even been involved in the project, became a fundamental stakeholder. With this new approach, IT was no longer the project sponsor, nor a position taken by the company's top management or even its president.

The project success indicators (originally printing volume and cost reduction) now also included: the total number of trees preserved; energy savings throughout the process, including basic raw material production such as paper, ink, and pieces of equipment; the reduced volume of water used in paper production; and reduced CO_2 emissions in the entire process. The overall approach to engage the entire company was redefined.

To maximize engagement by stakeholders from all company areas, a "green seal" was created to be given to the departments that achieved their printing reduction goals. Each director's office would receive its "green seal" only when all of its departments had received theirs.

Thus, a project that had the potential to be a nuisance and create discomfort was fully redirected to create collective commitment without losing sight of its objective of reducing costs, and, in addition, added a noble and moving purpose with strong popular appeal.

This is an excellent example of the importance of taking change management into account right from the project's initial planning phase. It was an *Information Technology project,* but not a project *of the Information Technology Department.* Conducted using a change management strategic approach, the project became a corporate endeavor aligned with strategic objectives.

Without a detailed evaluation of the stakeholders, opposing forces, and level of discomfort the proposed change would create, the purpose, identity, sponsor and engagement approach would have been different. And the results, for sure, would not have been the same.

1.10. Project Management or Organizational Transformation?

For many project managers and project management offices, a successful project is a project that is completed within the planned schedule, budget, and scope. Others may talk about achieving strategic objectives but that is all; they do not actually measure them and sustain them over time. However, after additional reflection, the previous perspective may change.

Consider the perspective of the company owner or top management who approves the project portfolio and the investments to be made. What do they really want after all?

Undoubtedly, we can answer that each project is a step in the transformation of an organization looking for differentiators to remain competitive, productive, and profitable. The factor that justifies the investment is the return it will bring to the organization.

Measuring a project using only technical parameters is a classic mistake that many companies still make. Measuring the outcome of a project immediately after it is completed is another issue requiring reconsideration. Nothing guarantees that the change will be sustainable and fully consolidated in the organizational culture over time.

Always keep in mind that, without people, there are no projects. While projects have a deadline for completion, the inclusion of a new way of working in an organization depends much more on the engagement of human beings than on the simple implementation of a new technology, process, or organizational redesign.

A project may indeed be completed within the planned timeframe, cost, scope, or quality and still bring little or no benefit for organizational transformation. It sounds simple, but the success of a project must be measured through parameters that do not end with the end of the project. Rather, the project's success must be measured through its ability to sustain itself over time and indeed transform an organization.

Those who decide about financial investments do not just want projects; they want organizational transformation. Projects are the only means to achieve that—hence the great importance we give to sustaining the change until it is actually assimilated.

Once again, change management needs to be strategic in nature. People's interest and engagement in the outcome of the project will determine the result of the undertaking. The true results cannot be seen right after completion of a project, but only over time, through quantitative and qualitative measurements of the proposed change.

We still have a lot to learn about project management. The easiest part to deal with is software, hardware, or redesign of the organizational structure and processes. The challenge is to promote an organizational transformation through projects that require managing the human dimension of the expected change in order to be successful.

Chapter 2

HCMBOK®—Human Change Management Body of Knowledge

The HCMBOK® is a methodology and a set of practices and tools based on various disciplines, including project management, anthropology, psychology, thanatology, people management, and leadership, and can be linked to any project management methodology. For didactic purposes and better understanding by the reader, the HCMBOK® provides a sequential view of the typical phases of a project. We hope this approach will facilitate the correlation of each macro-activity with a particular phase of the project.

In some project management methodologies, the acquisition phase is incorporated into the execution phase. Here we separated it out for didactic reasons, since, under the change management point of view, there are specific macro-activities to be developed in this phase.

Although HCMBOK®'s sequential structure of presentation may seem to connect it exclusively to traditional software development methodologies, also known as "cascade" or "waterfall," Figure 2.1 shows that its application fits perfectly into the agile methodologies through the accelerated performance of several cycles of acquisition, execution, implementation, and closing, each addressing a defined set of functionalities.

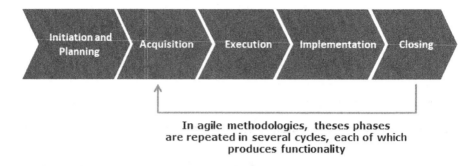

Figure 2.1   Phases repeated in agile methodology.

2.1. HCMBOK® Structure

Every project is by definition a temporary undertaking to deliver a new product, service, or exclusive result (*PMBOK® Guide, Fifth Edition*, 2013a). Projects have a clearly defined beginning and end. Most project management methodologies interpret as "end" the date on which the project is implemented or concluded.

However, organizational change does not follow this pattern. Each human being processes change in a different way. And many tend to resist it and, if possible, return to the state before the change, remaining in their comfort zone.

So, we added into the figure that represents HCMBOK®'s structure an additional phase, after the conclusion of the project, which we called *Production*. In this phase the change has been implemented, but it needs to be sustained until it is fully assimilated.

Some macro-activities presented in the following pages are typical of a specific phase; others are recurring (they begin in the planning phase and extend even beyond project completion). Regardless of the project management methodology to be adopted, we believe that proper application of HCMBOK® requires flexibility, both in the selection of the activities to be developed and the order in which such activities will be performed. The numbering does not imply sequential referencing. For example, in some cases, completing macro-activity 3.4 first can be important for obtaining better results in macro-activity 3.1.

Project phases themselves are often partially concurrent. It is important to be flexible; for example, a macro-activity in the execution phase maybe carried out along with other macro-activities in the planning phase.

The reader should understand that the HCMBOK® structure we use, with phases, macro-activities, and activities, is basically for didactic purposes and is not a rigid sequence that cannot be adjusted to the needs of each project.

We must also remind you that not all projects will require the use of all the macro-activities and activities. Establish your change management approach

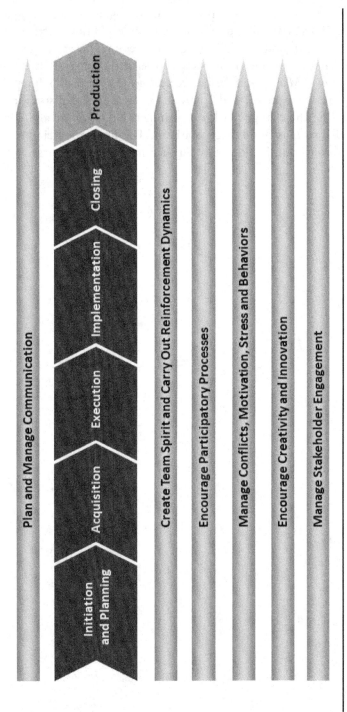

Figure 2.2 Macro view of the methodology that is part of the HCMBOK®.

(A description of Figure 2.2 can be found on the following page.)

by selecting those that best fit your project and are aligned with your organizational culture. If necessary, do not hesitate to include additional activities. The HCMBOK® is a guide and should be adjusted as required by each project.

Figure 2.2 illustrates the macro view of the methodology that is part of *The Human Change Management Body of Knowledge* (HCMBOK®). It represents the typical phases of a project and a *production phase,* included specifically to require sustaining the change until it is assimilated. The figure also contains macro-activities, such as Build Team Spirit and Use Dynamic Reinforcement, which occur throughout the project rather than in one specific phase.

Chapter 3

Project Initiation and Planning

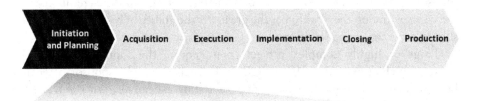

Project initiation and planning is the phase during which the organizational change management strategic approach should be defined, which can sometimes even influence the way the project will be organized and developed. The joint development of this phase with the project leaders enables alignment and integration from the early stage of the project. At the end of this phase, the Change Management Strategic Plan should be ready and approved. In addition, the action plan with operational tactics and activities should also be ready and integrated with the project's schedule of activities.

Here are the macro-activities that are part of this phase of the project.

3.1. Define and Prepare the Sponsor of the Project

Every change process needs a sponsor, someone with credibility and power to drive the change, monitor it, and intervene whenever necessary.

The sponsor is an active person committed to the change and ultimately responsible for its purpose and objectives. The sponsor's activities can be intense, especially in communication, conflict management, and stakeholder engagement management.

The sponsor must understand well his or her role and be available to work on the project. A good practice is to involve the sponsor by discussing his or her views on the project, the objectives to be achieved, the expectations regarding benefits, and the impacts from the project. In general, the sponsor will have participated in discussions about the changes that will be made. The sponsor must have a previous perception of the people, their positions, and areas that need to be involved. Discussing all these aspects and capturing the sponsor's perception is part of his or her preparation to act as a change agent, particularly important in organizations whose culture has not yet incorporated the practice of having sponsors who are active in organizational change. The greater the credibility of the sponsor among the workforce, the greater is the ability of his or her sponsorship to drive the change process.

Large or highly complex projects may require the sponsorship of the company's chief executive officer (CEO). In such cases, the sponsorship can be extended to a committee, a group of senior executives, with sufficient representation to support the change when the leading sponsor cannot be operationally involved.

This committee should have a sponsor-supported coordinator to make immediate decisions. Ideally, all members of the committee should be at the same hierarchical level. The coordinating function is used precisely to avoid

Figure 3.1 Sponsorship alternatives.

ego clashes in the committee. The coordinator is the one who "orders together" and therefore does not give a hierarchical weight to this position in the committee. However, even in these cases, the sponsor should be responsible for the initial communication of the vision for the future state of the organization after the changes are implemented, the purpose of the changes, and the goals and expectations. These actions ensure that his or her sponsorship is relentless, even if at times, a committee with senior representation performs that role. Figure 3.1 illustrates alternatives to having only one individual playing the sponsorship role.

We can say that, except in exceptional cases, a project should have only one sponsor. When you have two or more sponsors, their constant alignment is required in order to prevent mixed messages from reaching other stakeholders.

Even if you have a sponsor, in large or highly complex projects, co-sponsorship of other senior stakeholders will always be needed. The desired situation is that leaders at all levels are engaged and "sell" the change to their teams.

Whenever possible, sponsorship should not change during the project. The effects of a change can greatly affect the engagement of stakeholders, especially if the successor's style is different from that of his or her predecessors.

The worst situation we can imagine is that the sponsor, whether the same since the beginning of the project or a replacement, does not demonstrate engagement in the change. In our careers as consultants, we have seen cases where the sponsor acted as the main boycotter of the project. In these cases, the best approach to follow is to revisit the relevance of the change in relation to the company's strategy. There is little chance that the project will achieve its strategic objectives, and canceling it will be less expensive than moving forward and creating an instance of failure in the transformation of the organization. In many cases, unnecessary costs will be accumulated in addition to not achieving the planned benefits.

It is also necessary to take into account the impact that project failure because of lack of sponsorship will have on future endeavors. The organizational culture may create or reinforce the myth that the changes are not desired or acceptable. Even worse, the negative impression becomes one that, once started, projects cannot be suspended or canceled, even if they are not aligned with the strategic guidelines.

Many projects do not achieve their strategic objectives because of lack of engaged sponsorship. Data from PMI's report, *Pulse of the Profession® In-Depth Report: Executive Sponsor Engagement—Top Driver of Project and Program Success* (PMI, 2014c), show that "poorly engaged executive sponsors are the primary cause of projects not meeting goals significantly more often for low-performing organizations (43 percent versus 23 percent). High performers waste 10 times less money on projects than low performers due to poorly engaged sponsors."

Activities

> ➢ Define the sponsor of the project.
> ➢ Ensure the sponsor's commitment to, and availability for, the project.
> ➢ Prepare the sponsor to act in the project.
> ➢ Discuss the objective of the project, expectations, people, and areas that will be involved according to the sponsor's view.
> ➢ Identify the preliminary impacts perceived by the sponsor.
> ➢ Make sure that the sponsor is willing to face the challenges and be available to carry out the project:
>   ○ Evaluate the need to form a committee (sponsoring committee) to replace the sponsor when necessary;
>   ○ Define the coordinator of the committee and prepare him or her to act as a representative of the sponsor.

3.2. Hold a Working Session to Align and Mobilize Leaders

Many organizations that are beginning to apply a structured approach to organizational change management still need to raise their leaders' awareness of what this approach is, what it does, and what to expect from it.

Use a working session to present and educate participants regarding the importance of managing the process of change so that the strategic objectives that motivated the endeavor are achieved. In organizations where the practice of managing change is already institutionalized in the organizational culture, it is not necessary to spend time introducing the process to the leaders.

The leaders involved in the planned change must be aligned with the strategic objectives to be achieved. Although these objectives have been discussed' previously during the development of the strategic plan, the objectives of change projects are not always totally clear to everyone. Do not miss the opportunity to leave this event with the objective set out in a clear and compelling statement. The vision of the organization's future state after the change must also be clearly defined and aligned with all of the leaders. It is important to relate the project vision to the strategic plan, the objective of the project, the business plan, vision, mission, values, and culture of the organization.

This working session also serves to adjust expectations of leaders as well as clearly defining the metrics and goals to be achieved with the change project.

These metrics will be an important source to evaluate the assimilation of the change after its implementation and may have not only a qualitative but also, and mainly, a quantitative nature.

Projects that were preceded by feasibility studies or business plans with parameters—for example, profitability and productivity gains, ROI (return on investment), etc.—should use these data as references to be discussed and confirmed in the establishment of quantitative metrics.

Because the people involved in this working session are usually very busy, be pragmatic and develop it in a maximum of two hours, if possible in one hour.

One of the goals to be discussed is the time required to develop the project. In our consulting work, we have seen many projects die on the vine because they defined implementation goals that were totally out of touch with reality.

A few years ago, we worked on an enterprise resource planning (ERP) deployment project whose deadline was estimated by the vendor without taking into account input from the project team. The investments being negotiated were rather difficult, requiring significant discounts from the vendors. This led to a reduction of consulting services activities, so the implementation date was artificially anticipated.

The strategic objectives included the reduction of personnel costs through the automation of several business processes. This would require effort in redesigning the processes and training activities. It was not just a replacement of obsolete technology, but a change with high impact on processes and people. In addition, the system database to be replaced had several inconsistencies and outdated information. This implied a parallel project to make adjustments to the database. In spite of that, the board did not take into account suggestions for reviewing the implementation deadline presented by the project management team and instead the date suggested by the vendor.

The project team knew that, even by hiring new professionals and working overtime, the stipulated deadline was not feasible. Under great stress and feeling discredited for not having their opinion taken into account, the project team's engagement was far from what was necessary. Over the initial months some business processes were redesigned. However, as the priority was the deadline, several processes that could be optimized were left to be reviewed in a future project. The training schedule was also reduced. The result: Despite all the work carried out on holidays and weekends, after three months the vendor suggested that the project team had provided poor performance and proposed to postpone the date of implementation. Not only the estimated cost and the deadline, but also the strategic objectives, were affected. Several opportunities for improvements in business processes were delayed due to the pressure to complete the project by a deadline that was never understood and accepted by the project team.

If the project team does not believe in the goals, especially those related to its own deadlines, the project is not likely to be successful. It is more likely that the team will be overloaded and working on the verge of stress, and that motivation will be low. The leaders will be frustrated, the budget will be insufficient, and the culture will suffer an organizational scar, leaving a negative legacy in its wake.

In such cases, refer to benchmarks, data, and facts that show a logical sequence for developing the structured activities in a macro-schedule.

In the case presented above, studies of the average time to implement similar systems from independent sources and visits to companies that had already undergone the same type of project could help to define a project plan that would show, based on facts, a schedule able to realistically balance costs, scope, and time, in order to achieve the strategic objectives that motivated the investment.

Once the objective and goals of the project are defined, the organizational impacts preliminarily expected by the participants of the working session can be mapped. The leaders' perceptions of the organization related to the effects of the change are an important reference that will serve as input when performing the detailed mapping of the organizational impacts.

The project may not have formally started, but the workforce will eventually take notice of the mobilizing efforts to implement the change. To avoid speculation about a project that is in the planning phase, the best approach is to use the working session to define what will be communicated and how. Only in this way will the leaders leave the working session with one and the same message and set of behaviors about the change project. Communication of change must take into account the vision of the future state of the organization and the purpose of the change. Depending on the impact of the project, these items can be defined in this working session.

For better understanding by the reader, we will address the definition of the purpose in a specifically developed macro-activity.

Start the communication as soon as possible. Do not allow time for speculation. Remember, in the minds of the workforce, with or without public announcement, the project has already begun. If the sponsor has not yet been defined, this working session may serve as a forum to choose him or her.

This is also an excellent time to raise leaders' awareness of their role as active agents of change. Make it clear that the change needs support from the leaders of the organization to permeate the other organizational layers, not only during the development of the project, but also after its implementation, when the change needs to be sustained until it is assimilated.

Even if the leaders are aligned and apparently committed to the proposed change, perception of loss, changes in the chain of power, or even ego-related issues can affect some of these leaders. Use this opportunity to observe behaviors and evaluate potential antagonists.

When discomfort and resistance are obvious, tactics to mitigate this undesired situation should be further discussed with the sponsor in order to prevent this hidden force from opposing the change, affecting the engagement of other stakeholders.

Major organizational changes may require working sessions with involvement of all the high-ranking executives of the company. In this case it is best to hold the session external to any physical location of the organization in order to stay focused and generate the perception of criticality and mobilization to sustain the change. Use technological resources such as video conference to allow the participation of those who are in other geographic regions.

A successful working session is one that not only generates alignment but mainly *mobilizes the leaders* to drive the change project forward.

Activities

- ➤ Plan the working session to align and mobilize the leaders, and review it with the project manager and sponsor.
- ➤ Introduce the organizational change management approach and its relevance for the success of the project, regardless of whether or not this is the first instance of change management for the organization.
- ➤ Align the vision for the future state of the organization and project objectives. Define goals and quantitative and qualitative metrics. The latter must be aligned with the business plan and strategy of the organization.
- ➤ Define the strategy to communicate the change and communicate it as soon as possible.
- ➤ Raise the leaders' awareness of their role as active agents of change (co-sponsors).
- ➤ Observe behaviors and evaluate potential antagonists or sellers of change.

3.3. Define the Project's Purpose and Identity

The objective of a change is its major motivating factor, a compelling sentence indicating what will be changed. For example, if an IT function will be outsourced, the driver could be cost reduction through economies of scale. This objective, however, is linked to other relevant change drivers such as focus on the target activity of the business and improvement in the quality of the outsourced function, among others.

For the purpose of the change, there is a deeper and more comprehensive way to promote the objective to be achieved. While the objective brings an understanding of the change in the rational sense, that is, "what" will be changed, the purpose touches the emotions, that is, "why" the change will occur.

Creating a purpose represents not only the objective, but also the stakeholders' perspective, and this requires an empathic attitude from the change manager. We need to look, and feel, the effects of the change from the point of view of those it will affect. This is the only way it will be possible to define a purpose that can really give meaning to the change, expand the possibility of engagement, and facilitate communication as well as provide an understanding of the intended change.

In the example provided, it can be anticipated that the stakeholders whose functions will be outsourced will likely feel the loss of emotional ties with their organization unless an adequate change management approach is used. It is likely that resistance will be high, affecting even those employees whose functions will not be outsourced. The primary objective is the true target of outsourcing, but if there is no purpose capable of promoting the change from the human, or emotional, point of view, people will feel outsourced as if they themselves were things—disposable objects.

By reflecting more carefully on the planned change, it is evident that the main objective will bring about positive effects, realizable only with the proper focus. The purpose of the change cannot lose sight of the objective, but it can include a more complete and human approach in the proposed communication.

In this particular case, the employees who are now part of the outsourced company will begin working in an organization whose main activity is their respective expertise. Learning and development opportunities will certainly be greater in a company with these activities. Moreover, cost optimization and improved quality of support functions may increase the organization's competitiveness, creating new development opportunities for the business and its workforce. Even the customers can benefit from this initiative.

If the purpose is defined from this standpoint, the change, although producing an inevitable perception of pain in some people, will benefit many stakeholders. Without losing sight of this primary objective, the change will obtain greater engagement, the period of pain and feeling of loss will be shorter, and there will be less suffering for all.

All change must have a purpose capable of placing peoples' beings, not just their bodies, in the change movement. Change initiatives without a clear purpose easily understood by the stakeholders are doomed to low engagement, will cause great organizational distress, or even fail.

The purpose is an important part of the change communication strategy and can be set by the sponsor together with the project management team or by the leaders during the working session for alignment and mobilization for the change, especially in projects that will have a strong impact on the organization.

To summarize, we can say that the purpose has to do with "why" the change will be made, the objective is related to "what" will be changed, and the planning of the change project has to do with "how" the change will be made.

Figure 3.2 shows the three change communication elements and the order in which they should be communicated—why we will make the change, what we will change, and how we will change it.

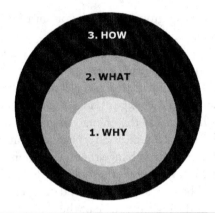

Figure 3.2   Communication elements and order.

Once the purpose of the change is defined, the project requires an identity, a name, a slogan, and an image (logo) that together clearly communicate and provide branding for the implementation efforts.

There are cases where the project requires an identity from its initial planning, which prevents the use of a participatory process involving several stakeholders. A meaningful alternative is to allow the project team or other stakeholders to take part in identity development. This participatory approach helps to increase team identification with the project and can be performed as one of the kick-off activities. In this case, direct involvement of stakeholders in the definition of identity will have a positive effect on the sense of belonging and engagement in the change project.

Several years ago, we worked on a project to implement a new commercial system. The organization worked 24 hours per day, 365 days per year. In this context, stopping the operation to implement the system was a real challenge. The project identity was built using the image of a "pit stop" in car races, representing a quick stop to make the adjustments that would allow for greater competitiveness and a fresh start toward excellence. We also added to the project logo a slogan to reinforce the message of the expected changes: "Race for excellence."

Activities

➢ Define the purpose of the change.
➢ Define and brand the project's identity.

3.4. Mapping and Classifying Stakeholders

A stakeholder is any person, group of people, or entity that will be directly or indirectly affected by the change.

The *Stakeholder Map* is one of the main change management support tools. It is highly confidential and available only to the project management team. It is where the stakeholders are identified and classified in accordance with their positioning in relation to the change. Using this tool, project managers can detect potential conflicts, assess the change management effort with greater accuracy, as well as define communication strategies to interact with antagonists to understand their anxieties and change their perception of the change project.

The Stakeholder Map is a dynamic tool that is fundamental for change management. It should be re-evaluated and updated periodically, as behavioral changes in stakeholders during the course of the project are relatively common.

There are many types of stakeholder maps. Because it is simple and easy to use, we chose the type described in the following pages and illustrated in Figure 3.3.

The map should be developed in a participatory manner by the entire project management team so that different perspectives and convergent perceptions can be identified. The classification of stakeholders is a speculative process that must take into account the preliminary point of view of the sponsor, and the data collected during the working session for the leaders as well as the team's perception. As the project evolves, the behavior of the stakeholders will allow for a more precise classification.

A good practice is to promote frequent interactions with stakeholders, especially those with high power and influence in project decisions. Each of these interactions is an opportunity to assess expectations, behaviors, and the level of engagement. These topics will be discussed in detail in Chapters 13 and 15, on behavior management and stakeholder engagement management.

The revision of the Stakeholder Map should be one of the activities of the meetings of the project management team, which usually are held every week or every two weeks. The project management team should be trained to observe behaviors in each interaction with stakeholders and may propose updates to the map at any time.

Stakeholder Map

Stakeholder/Profile	Decision-Making Stakeholder	Direct Influencing Agent	Indirect Influencing Agent	Spectator
Employee A	Seller			
Employee B		Probable Resistant Stakeholder		
Employee C			Open Boycotter	
X Team	Supporter			
Y Team				Unstable Stakeholder
Z Team		Veiled Boycotter		

Figure 3.3 Stakeholder Map tool.

Large-scale projects can have hundreds of stakeholders. In this case, where possible, begin by listing stakeholders by groups, for example, sales team, VIP customers, department X. Avoid listing too many people, because the management of a map with dozens of stakeholders will not be productive. During the project, it is likely that it will be necessary to classify stakeholders into groups with different behaviors, which will require that the original group be broken down into subgroups or even individuals. Focus on those stakeholders who are a priority and who will have more influence on the project; create a list just for them.

Updating this tool is important so that you are able to monitor how the project is evolving in relation to engagement of the stakeholders. Even more important is to plan and develop actions to manage the stakeholders using these updated lists.

Activities

> Promote frequent interactions with stakeholders and assess their expectations, behaviors, and their level of engagement.
> List everyone who is either directly or indirectly involved in the change, including those both inside and outside of the organization; determine whether they will be approached individually or as a group.
> Classify them according to the following criteria described in the following section:
>   o Capacity to influence project decisions and direction.
>   o Probable change supporters and nonsupporters.

Capacity to Influence Project Decisions and Direction

☐ **Decision-making stakeholders.** They are the main players in the project's decision-making process. Their engagement and commitment are crucial for the success of the proposed change; sponsors are, by definition, decision makers. Not necessarily all of the decision-making stakeholders are senior leaders, but quite often people who have power are found under this classification.

☐ **Direct influencing agents.** They do not have the power to decide, but they directly influence project direction and mood, especially when working closely with the decision-making stakeholders.

❑ **Indirect influencing agents.** They do not have the power to decide but can influence the project by acting behind the scenes. They are opinion makers and, if they have a persuasive profile, they may have significant impact on other stakeholders' engagement. They usually influence the direct influencing agents, but we will often find within their ranks those who are connected with decision-making stakeholders and can also influence them.

❑ **Spectators.** They will experience the change and may boycott it, but they cannot change the project result by acting alone. However, a relevant number of opposing spectators can create complications in the change production phase. In fact, spectators should not be classified individually but as a group or entity. In a project to build a port, for example, a worker alone is a spectator, powerless to affect the project. However, as a united group, workers can go on strike and stop the work under way, causing serious financial losses and compromising the schedule.

Probable Change Supporters and Nonsupporters

❑ **Sellers.** They support and sell the project naturally and are proud to participate. Every sponsor should, by definition, be the major seller of the project.

❑ **Supporters.** They will support the change provided that they clearly understand their purpose in it.

❑ **Unstable stakeholders.** This classification is common at the beginning of a project, when a stakeholder's position is not yet clear. Lack of positioning is the typical behavior of this type of stakeholder. He or she is unable to decide whether to support or resist the change. A specific strategy should be developed for these stakeholders, looking for ways to increase possibilities for their engagement before they take a position antagonistic to the project. Usually, no stakeholder keeps this position as the project evolves, except those who joined the project when it was already under way.

❑ **Probable resistant stakeholders.** These are stakeholders who cannot yet be classified. Their signals are not clear as those of the stakeholders classified as "unstable." However, their background, personal style, or the impact of the change on their activities allow us to infer that they will probably resist the change. Special attention should also be given in these cases to reduce the possibility that they will turn into antagonists as the project develops.

❏ **Open boycotters.** Stakeholders who do not hide their dissatisfaction and openly resist the change.

❏ **Veiled boycotters.** These stakeholders seem to have adhered, but they resist behind the scenes. This type of stakeholder is the worst type. They require special attention because they can undermine the project without the manager noticing. They usually remain in this veiled position for a long time and then become more active after the project is completed, making change assimilation and institutionalization more difficult. The typical behavior of this type of stakeholder is to try to re-establish his or her comfort zone by going back to the processes, tools, and techniques used before the change. Veiled boycotters' positioning before the sponsor and project management team is usually inconsistent with their behavior.

3.5. Assess Characteristics of the Organizational Culture and Its Effects on the Change Efforts

Every organization has a unique organizational culture, that is, a set of customs, habits, beliefs, values, and behaviors usually accepted and used—an unspoken way of doing things within the particular organization. Note that, in many cases, the culture does not fully coincide with what the organization states formally in its values, beliefs, mission, and vision.

Culture is the result of what is done, not of what is said. That is why the attitude of leaders is a major influencing component in the formation of a culture. The leaders' influence is such that sometimes a simple change of leaders directly impacts organizational culture or subculture and, consequently, the behavior of the humans working there.

Another element that has strongly influenced culture shaping is the way the company conducts its people management processes—how it selects, hires, receives, and integrates a new employee; and how it evaluates, promotes, recognizes, punishes, fires, and rewards people, in its broadest sense, including benefits and variable compensation (for example, bonuses for results).

Even if the organization has common cultural traits, every department can have its own cultural characteristics, just as a country has a national culture and regional subcultures.

The evaluation of the characteristics of the organizational culture provides preliminary insight into the impacts the change may cause. The more the change affects cultural paradigms, the greater is the probability of resistance. Many changes are reflected in the culture, and these are the ones that require additional management effort and longer change assimilation periods.

Imagine a culture that recognizes seniority as a status differentiator among its workforce. Older employees are often treated as heroes and references of success. They enjoy small privileges and feed on the admiration of others. In companies with this characteristic, knowledge of the details of every business process and the network of interpersonal relations is usually highly valued.

Now imagine that the organization must undergo technological modernization in order to remain competitive. With technology, new and more modern business processes will be implemented.

At face value, what changes is the technology and the way that business processes are operationalized. However, the real change will take place in the people and the culture: Power structures will be broken; prominent figures will lose status and privileges; the security of knowledge and know-how acquired over decades will be replaced by the uncertainty of the new—creating potential resistance to the change.

The less resilient individuals will feel devalued as a result of the losses mentioned above. For a time, they will denounce the benefits of the change and try to retain the advantages of the previous model. It is quite likely that not everyone will be able to adapt to the new reality. Some will have to be transferred to other functions, or, in the extreme, dismissed from the company.

If normal employee termination is a factor of stress and demotivation and creates a state of grieving, in this cultural context, the proposed change will demand an even more careful change management approach so that the transition from the previous state to the new one is the shortest and smoothest possible.

Although the effect of the change in this culture poses a risk, it also presents an opportunity. People known for their prior knowledge can be involved in decision making through participatory processes, reducing their resistance and the perception of cultural eruption. They can also act as references in the transition from tacit knowledge, the internal knowledge of each person that was not shared through any means, to explicit knowledge, which is shared among people, codified, accessed, and documented through whatever means. Ultimately, their differentiated status in the group can be co-opted rather than being pushed to the background, in order to promote these people's engagement and appreciation. Their recognition as a source of knowledge in the workforce can be harnessed if they are assigned to improve the new operating model.

In this case, assessment of the cultural characteristics will reveal the effects of the change and help to plan the actions that can turn a potentially risky situation into one of engagement.

The change management strategy must be fully aligned with the organizational culture. In cases of change that affect an organization in different geographic regions or worldwide, consider the implications of a regional or country culture. Studies show that the culture of a region, and especially of a country, has a strong influence on organizational culture. Certainly, change management approaches in a global organization such as Honda will be somewhat different for the same project affecting countries such as Brazil or Japan, due to the cultural differences.

The assessment of organizational culture should observe explicit and tacit factors. Values and beliefs, for example, have an explicit side, (formally documented) and a tacit one (undeclared). Both are part of the organizational culture.

Recently, a Brazilian media company dismissed a journalist while he was on vacation out of the country. Several employees learned of his dismissal, and as the journalist was well liked, they posted messages of solidarity and support on the social media. However, the fired journalist had not been informed of his new situation, which happened soon afterward, through an email. The aggravating factor is that in the Brazilian culture this is a great offense, as layoffs are usually made in person. Interestingly, "respect for the human being" was one of the values of this company that for years had led an organizational climate project to try to be on the list of best companies for which to work. Shortly afterward the company carried out several similar actions, further widening the gap between speech and practice, explicit and tacit cultural attributes.

In this example we see that, although "respect for the human being" is one of the company's stated values, the institutionalized belief in the organization is that it uses and discards people without consideration. This discrepancy in the organizational culture can only be perceived, through formal interviews and informal conversations, by someone who is not part of the company—when and if that person is able to build trust and credibility with the workforce.

There is a lot to be learned about a company's culture from explicit elements. Observe the physical environment. Are there areas for socializing? Do the employees' work areas have personal elements, such as family photos, for example, or are they standardized and depersonalized?

Are the bathrooms clean as expected in the regional culture? If the regional culture is particularly concerned with hygiene, and the bathrooms are not cleaned adequately, it is clear that the human question is not being treated as expected by the workforce.

The macro-activity of assessing the organizational culture demands formal investigation not only through interviews and observation but also through more informal approaches involving the workforce.

We were once on a consulting job in a company that appeared to us immediately to be highly hierarchical, giving employees little voice. This cultural trait would hinder the application of participatory processes because everyone would be conditioned to obey and not give opinions and to follow instructions but not participate in the proposed change. The description of the culture articulated by the leaders (that theirs was a participatory culture) was inconsistent with what we observed. We asked to visit the common areas. When we reached the parking lot, we observed that there was an area specified for directors, another for managers, and finally a common area. The dining hall was divided into two parts—one for the executives and another for everyone else. On the company badges the departments were identified by colors. However, all executives, regardless of their area, had blue badges—a color not used by any department. The experience of observing explicit cultural elements confirmed our initial perceptions.

The tacit elements of this highly hierarchical culture made it clear that any small sign of sponsorship for the change would have a high impact on the workforce. At the same time, the risk of antagonism from a leader would easily influence the behavior of all of his or her subordinates.

The elements of the organizational culture can be used to support the change, but they can also make the engagement of stakeholders difficult. As we have said before, when you identify an element of the organizational culture during this activity, evaluate its effect on the planned change and describe the action that will have to be developed to support the change or to address possible negative effects that may reinforce antagonism.

Cultural elements can be factors of antagonism or engagement, depending on the situation. For example, an organization has cultural myths that (1) projects are never successful and (2) projects always have an impact on company operations. This organization must coordinate actions to debunk the myths. Communication must articulate clearly all of the actions that will be taken to ensure that the project in question has a result that is different from the expected negative result.

Some time ago we consulted on a project in an organization where this myth was part of the culture. Various previous projects had shaped and reinforced this myth over the years. Projects were carried out without the direct involvement of the people who would make use of the deliverables (products, services, and results) developed by the project. So we implemented an activity to eliminate the effect of this myth—integrating operational areas with the project. A council was assembled, composed of leaders from the areas represented, so these leaders could express their opinions and recommendations and feel they were an active part of the outcome. People from the operating areas began to be involved in all the changes made during the execution phase, even going on international trips to observe similar projects. The result was surprising—a myth with a negative perspective was replaced by the belief that projects should always provide integration with the operating areas.

Every project is an opportunity to shape elements of the organizational culture. The alignment of change management with Human Resources can leverage available opportunities and give rise to a culture that is managed, not the result of what is happening randomly in the organization.

Extreme cases that pose a threat to the success of the venture should also be included in the project Risk Map. This map is not a change management tool; it is a project management tool. However, the risks inherent in human affairs must also be listed in it and monitored.

Organizational culture has a strong influence on some recurring macro-activities such as communication planning, creation of team spirit, encouragement

Table 3.1. Aspects of Organizational Culture to Be Observed

Beliefs and assumptions	Most times, beliefs and assumptions are hidden perceptions; they are what is believed and what is accepted as truth, without being formally stated by the company.
Values	Formal statement of what the company preaches, for example, "respect for people." Many times there is no direct correlation between what is stated and what is done.
Myths	What is told about the history of the company, whether or not it is true. It is often a distorted interpretation of the reality over time.
Language and communication symbols	All the elements that communicate something. They range from the most traditional (bulletin boards, logos, slogans) to symbols of power and prominence (furniture, room size, colors used, etc.).
Ceremonies and rituals	Events regularly carried out in the organization to give more visibility to its culture, ratifying values and strengthening myths and beliefs.
Taboos—both tacit and explicit	Practices and customs unacceptable within the organization. Some are included in the company standards, others are tacit—they are part of the belief of what is not desirable in organizational behaviors.
Standards and formalities	The explicit conduct and behavior rules of an organization.
Heroes	Players who have left their marks on the company's history. In a way, they represent the current culture or the idealized past.
Attitude of leadership	This is the actual behavior of the leaders. It does not have to do with what is said but with what is done. It is the example, not the words or formal behaviors that count.
People management practices	This is how the company hires, dismisses, promotes, evaluates, recognizes, and compensates people, in its broader sense, including benefits and variable compensation (giving bonuses for results).

of creativity and innovation, application of participatory processes, conflict management, behaviors, motivation and stress, and, especially, stakeholder engagement management.

Table 3.1 identifies and describes the main components of an organization that should be observed when assessing its culture.

Activities

> ➤ Circulate throughout the company and observe the physical environment, assessing the explicit and tacit elements of the culture.
> ➤ Conduct formal interviews and informal conversations with the stakeholders; diagnose the organizational culture.
> ➤ Evaluate the cultural elements and list them as factors of antagonistic to or engaged in the planned change.
> ➤ Evaluate and list the risks posed by the cultural characteristics on the planned change and include these human factor risks in the project Risk Map.
> ➤ Develop a plan to manage the effects of the organizational culture on the change and discuss it with the project leaders.

3.6. Define the Roles and Responsibilities of the Project Team

3.6.1. Prepare the RACI (Responsible, Accountable, Consulted, and Informed) Matrix

Clear understanding of the role of each person involved in the project, either directly or indirectly, is an essential step to promote engagement in the purpose of the change and to reduce tension among stakeholders. Conflicts may arise from a dispute about carrying out a particular activity that two stakeholders each consider his or her responsibility. Even worse is to have an activity not carried out because no one was clearly assigned to perform it.

Failure to define each stakeholder's or group of stakeholders' role(s) and responsibilities is almost always a cause for speculation and uncertainty, feeding antagonistic attitudes toward the project. No one engages in the unknown.

The Responsible, Accountable, Consulted, and Informed (RACI) Matrix, which is basically a tool for alignment of expectations and communication, is useful in defining roles and responsibilities. Figure 3.4 is an example of a completed RACI Matrix tool.

RACI Matrix				
Responsibility/ Activity	Stakeholder X	Stakeholder Y	Stakeholder Z	Committee
Definition of scope	A	R	I	C
Budget approval	R		R	A
Time management	R	I	A	C
Knowledge management	A	R		I
Hiring			R	A
Process approval	A	R	I	C
Implementation approval	C	C	C	A

Figure 3.4   Example of a RACI Matrix.

At this phase of the project, the RACI Matrix will be used to define roles and responsibilities of the project team, taking into account even the activities to sustain the change. In the execution phase of the project we will revise this matrix, focusing on the roles and responsibilities to be performed in the production phase, after the change has been implemented.

If possible, the matrix should be prepared in a participatory way in order to increase each stakeholder's commitment to his or her role. It must always be widely communicated in order to dispel any doubts.

Roles and responsibilities may change as projects develop. Keep the RACI Matrix updated all the time, and communicate any changes to your key stakeholders whenever you change it.

RACI Matrix Format

❑ On one axis, list stakeholders individually or by groups with the same roles.
❑ On the other axis, define the project's activities.
❑ Define the role of each stakeholder or group of stakeholders in each activity of the project in accordance with the following criteria:

○ *R – Responsible.* This stakeholder is not responsible for the final result of the activity but is responsible for ensuring that it is done. Therefore, he or she is the executor of the activity. Several stakeholders can be responsible for carrying out the same activity.

○ *A – Accountable.* This stakeholder is responsible for seeing that the macro-activity is completed. Whenever you identify more than one accountable stakeholder in an activity, check whether this activity should actually be divided into two separate activities. The objective is that just one stakeholder is accountable for a macro-activity.

○ *C – Consulted.* As the name indicates, this is the group of stakeholders who interact, listen and speak, is consulted, and has an active voice and can influence a particular decision.

○ *I – Informed.* This is the stakeholder who is merely informed about a particular action or activity. In spite of that, creating a feedback channel for each communication is a good practice.

NOTE: Not all of the fields in a RACI Matrix require completion. There are activities that involve only two or three people as well as others in which all participants will have to be classified as R, A, C, or I.

Activities

➤ List the activities that must be carried out by the project team.
➤ Define the RACI Matrix using a participatory process if possible.
➤ Widely communicate the RACI Matrix.
➤ Communicate updates whenever necessary.

3.6.2. Define the Project Organization Chart

This is also the time to determine the project management structure. Each project is unique, and organizational culture should be taken into account when defining its management structure. The structure should be depicted graphically in a Project Organization Chart (see Figure 3.5) for purposes of communicating the structure and defining how decision making will be done.

For the project to flow smoothly, the power of decision making and responsibilities of each level of the structure must be clear. The typical structure of most projects comprises the following components.

❑ **A steering committee.** A higher level of decision making, led by the project sponsor, who, ultimately, makes the decisions with the greatest impact on the organization and project. Usually, this committee monitors the project on a monthly basis, checking the overall status in terms of schedule, costs, scope, stakeholders' engagement, and any possible deviation of the change and project plan. Some major strategic issues presented by the project management committee may be discussed and decided.

❑ **A project management committee.** Coordinated by the project manager, this committee is formed by decision-making stakeholders, usually second-tier executives, who monitor the project and make the relevant tactical decisions. It is responsible for submitting the summary of project progress report to the steering committee and should include the decisions with greater organizational impact. Its formal management structure usually calls for weekly or biweekly meetings to revise and discuss the project progress report prepared by the project manager, considering: schedule, costs, scope, stakeholders' engagement, team motivation and stress level, incidence of conflicts, any possible change and project plan deviation, additional resources needed, trends, and preparation for next steps. This committee should also define the items that will be presented to the steering committee.

❑ **Project manager.** As one of three decision-making levels, the project manager is responsible for the tactical and operational decisions of the project. He or she usually prepares the project progress report to be discussed with the project management committee. This report should include the evolution of the schedule, costs, scope changes, project climate, stakeholders' engagement, and any other relevant information about the current project status and trends. The project manager should also be an influencing agent in strategic decisions made by the steering committee.

❑ **Project management team.** Very common in large, complex projects, this team supports the project manager in the management of variables such as schedule, cost, quality, integration, organizational change management, etc. For small projects, usually there will be no project management team. In such cases, all the tasks related to project management will be performed by the project manager alone.

❑ **Project development teams.** Coordinated by a team leader, these teams are formed by the executors of the project's activities related to business areas, such as process definitions. They are often organized according to departmental or functional capabilities and can have members from business areas and other departments such as IT, office of process design, and consultants.

Make the organizational structure as simple as possible. Three decision-making levels is more than enough for most projects. The higher the number of hierarchical levels for a project, the harder will be the decision-making process, which then favors the action of antagonists, who may request that a certain issue be analyzed at a higher level, no matter where the decision currently lies.

In some cases we have found that other stakeholders may be part of the project management structure, but if they are included, they usually overload the committees with too many members. Avoid having more than six or seven people on each committee.

In these cases, these are stakeholders who usually influence the project. Sometimes, they are professionals who are seen as a technical reference for an activity—the bastions of knowledge. When they are widely respected in the organization, their endorsement may influence engagement by other stakeholders. Not involving them may reinforce antagonism.

An effective alternative for getting their commitment to the project without the need for additional decision-making levels in the structure is to create parallel *councils,* as shown below in the Project Organization Chart in Figure 3.5.

The councils use participatory processes to give voice to these stakeholders. By creating a space for them to express their opinions and recommend actions for the project, emotions are not repressed, and they stay connected with the project. The perception of "being part of" (belonging) increases and infects other stakeholders who are not connected directly to the project team.

The meetings of the councils should be facilitated in such a way as to make the councilors speak more than listen. When they do not express their position, make them participate using direct questions and/or group dynamics.

Place any councils as parallel structures just below the project management committee so as not to create the impression that they are hierarchically under the project manager.

The call to create a council should come from the sponsor, to emphasize its importance and persuade the councilors to participate actively in the meetings.

A common reaction by antagonists who have been asked to be part of a council is not to attend the meetings or send representatives. Make the role of the council and the need for direct participation clear from the outset, emphasizing that representatives will only be allowed in exceptional cases.

Council and committee members tend to be busy people who may perceive the meetings as an additional activity in their agenda. Ensure that meetings do not last longer than one hour and are scheduled with the minimum possible frequency to reduce the impact on the councilors' daily activities.

Set all the dates and times of the meetings when you communicate the project management structure, so everyone can get organized and do not miss the meetings because of actual or alleged commitments.

Figure 3.5 is an example of a typical project management structure, which should always be adapted to the different cultural realities and levels of project complexity.

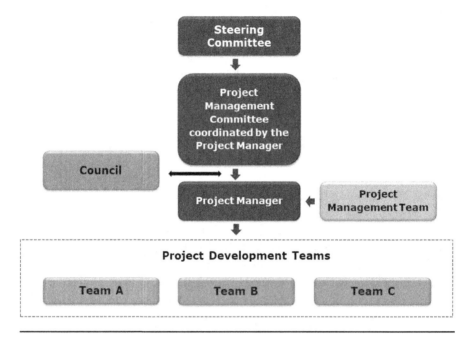

Figure 3.5 Project Organization Chart.

> **NOTE:** The meetings of committees and councils are excellent opportunities to observe behaviors and members' engagement with the change. A good practice is to conduct team debriefings of the meetings to gather the team's perceptions of each member's position. Update the stakeholder map after every meeting and define engagement actions or complementary approaches to understand the root cause of any possible discomfort with the change perceived by the project management team.

The criteria for defining the members of committees and councils should be clear. Special attention should be given to the creation of these structures.

Leaving out someone important may cause a perception of exclusion and foster antagonism. When communicating the members of the project management structure, be sure to communicate the criteria used, not only to the members, but also to those who will not participate.

Activities

- ➤ Define the project management structure and the operating rules
- ➤ Approve the project management structure with the Sponsor and communicate it to the stakeholders
- ➤ Define the project management structure agenda and communicate it
- ➤ Organize a meeting for the sponsor to communicate the project management structure.

3.7. Adjust the Physical Environment to the Project Needs

The issue of physical space during execution of a project is often considered not very important. It is not always possible to get the ideal space because of the physical limitations of the organization itself. However, the right physical environment can play a role in inspiration, motivation, and demonstration of the importance of the project. It helps to improve the project team's engagement. On the other hand, inadequate space may bring about negative effects of the same proportion.

There are instances where the team will be inevitably spread over different geographical regions. Define integration and communication rituals to maintain alignment and promote team spirit, despite the physical distance.

Virtual teams spread geographically demand even more attention to keep them integrated. A good practice is to have a large TV set with a full-time video conference structure in each place, simulating a window to keep teams virtually connected.

The priority is to ensure that at least all ergonomic and hygienic factors are fully met. The minimum comfort of the team's physical workspace, adequate temperature, clean restrooms, and good food are examples of requirements that, if not met, will strongly affect team motivation.

Even so, the change manager is responsible for evaluating the relevance of this issue for the success of the project and should include it in the budget (for example, the rental of a dedicated space for the project).

Take care not to turn the project into an "island" isolated from the organization. The physical distance between the project and the company's operating areas can increase this isolation, but it can also happen when the project management team does not communicate regularly with the workforce members who are not part of the project.

Table 3.2 shows positive and negative effects that the nature of the physical workspace can have on the project team.

Table 3.2. Effects from Adequate or Inadequate Physical Space

Adequate Physical Space	Inadequate Physical Space
Promotes integration and supports creation of team spirit	May generate unintended perception of higher or lower status
Facilitates communication	May generate distortions in verbal messages
Stimulates creativity	Discourages an inspiring environment
Generates a sense of belonging and identity	Makes creation of a common project identity more difficult
Confirms the relevance of the project	Promotes a perception of "lesser importance"
Generates the comfort necessary to reduce the effects of stress, affecting productivity positively	May be an additional factor of stress and stimulation of conflict, especially if minimum comfort conditions are not met

Activities

➤ Plan the appropriate physical environment for the project, ensuring that ergonomic and hygiene requirements are met.
➤ Estimate rental costs and/or any costs to adapt the environment and include them in the project budget.

3.8. Plan the Team's Assignment and Development

3.8.1. Team's Assignment and Postproject Assignment

In large projects, especially when people are transferred from their usual functions to be dedicated exclusively to a project, it is expected that they will have concerns about their future in the organization. There are professionals who have an established position in the company, and their leaders clearly demonstrate that these key peoples' position after the project is guaranteed, and that contract employees will replace them just for the timeframe of the project. In such cases, the leaders' commitment to the future of the employees is explicit, and the employees usually do not feel that their position in the organization is threatened. However, this is not always possible, because the function performed by these employees may disappear as a result of changes brought about by the project.

The future of those who participate full-time in a project can be as uncertain as that of those who do not participate. That is, the image and future of every employee in the organization depend heavily on their technical and behavioral performance in the present.

Projects are excellent opportunities to develop new skills that become part of every employee's career, in the present or in any other future situation. It is more likely for a project that generates staff reduction to affect those who are not working directly in it to a greater degree. The investment in the development of a high-performance team for a project tends to be maintained, even by reassigning people to another role in the organization.

However, keeping one's job is a priority for most people. It is important to deal with the issue of the project team members' futures *at the time they are assigned.* When it is not possible to guarantee that certain team members will keep their jobs after the project, coordinate with the company to offer special dismissal conditions, when necessary. Include the costs related to these conditions (extension of health insurance, bonuses, etc.) in the project budget. Communicate the possible scenarios to reduce the pressure of psychological insecurity and the possibility of the team going into the negative state of anticipatory grief. Show that, no matter the scenario, people will be treated with dignity.

Do not create expectations that you cannot sustain later. If something unforeseen occurs, organizational credibility, as well as your credibility, will be affected, jeopardizing the engagement of people in future projects.

Although there may be some uneasiness, when the organizational culture has already incorporated the belief that projects are career opportunities and that project members who are dismissed are treated with dignity, the team tends to feel safer from the moment they are appointed.

Usually the person required for the project is key in his or her area. Often, when an assignment is requested, those who have to give up employees release an employee whose contributions and expertise will be missed much less by that area. This person will hardly be the ideal resource for the project.

People are more interested in getting involved in projects when companies use a participatory management model and offer attractive and challenging goals and meaningful purpose. When the organizational culture recognizes learning and career opportunities within its projects, it is much easier to get volunteers. Sometimes, there will be more people interested in participating in the project than the project really needs.

In some instances, people have no choice when they are assigned to a project. However, it is good practice to approach the required team members and invite them to join the project. However, if the organization has not achieved this level of participatory management in its evolution and transformation through projects, approaching the team with an invitation may not be the best strategy. Should there be many refusals, you will eventually have to enforce participation. The strategy may backfire because people will ultimately realize that, in fact, they never had an option. If that happens, engagement will likely be lower, at least in the initial phase of the project.

In either of these cases (invitation or direct assignment), prepare an appropriate communication to the project participants that includes the purpose of the project, the word of the sponsor, and the challenges to be overcome. This is essential for people to accept the project positively, thus reducing potential antagonistic forces.

An organizational leader can also provide a complementary approach to direct and informal communication for those who may be unhappy with compulsory participation in the project. This direct contact helps in understanding the behavior of each individual, his or her fears, and alternatives for future engagement.

The care that must be given to the employees assigned to be part of a project must be extended as well to those who will not participate in it. The frustration of these stakeholders may affect their commitment to the change, bringing negative consequences in the future. When the criteria to select the project team are made clear, it is easier for those who were left out to accept the situation.

Monitoring the impacts related to the assignment of the project team, both on the members and on those who were left out, is a necessary approach in the management of stakeholders.

Activities

> Negotiate team allocation.
> Establish the commitment that project participants will be treated with dignity, in accordance with their performance and the opportunities within the organization.
> Invite or assign project participants.
> Monitor the motivation of the project members and the frustration of those who are not on the project.

3.8.2. Define and Implement Preliminary Training

Adequate up-skilling from the moment the team is allocated is another important factor to create motivation and encourage engagement in the project goals and objectives.

Even if an individual who has been assigned to the project has the desired technical profile and knowledge of the business, development of new competencies is often necessary for best project performance. Not all team members will have an understanding of the routine daily activities of a project. In addition, new technologies will demand that each individual is prepared for the new environment and/or new management approach of the business areas involved.

People who feel inadequate to face the challenges assigned to them will experience discomfort again. Just having to participate in the project is already a change in the lives of these people.

Defining a preliminary training plan for providing knowledge necessary for the project team to be successful reduces the chances that people will go into a negative state of anticipatory grief. The message that the project leaders are committed to providing the best possible conditions for the individual success of each project member will bring positive effects, creating a climate of psychological security and motivation.

Although it is not always possible to define the entire training plan at this stage of the project, the initial definition, in addition to anticipating needs, helps to moderate stress and make the team feel more comfortable with the new and unknown.

Failure to prepare the team for the project is the same as sending them out on a road trip without a GPS. The effect can be devastating; starting this activity too late will certainly cause project delays.

If the organization has a well-structured training and development department, involve this department as early in the project as possible. If this department does not exist, take on this role or consider hiring a company that specializes in learning design and development.

Change management is not an area of expertise exclusive to a small group of experts. On the contrary, the more people who are trained and prepared to develop change management activities, the better. Take this opportunity to train the project management team in the basic principles of change management. Remember, you will need support to evaluate the stakeholder behaviors and continually adjust the engagement and resistance reduction strategies. Training the project management team not only multiplies their action by providing a view of the human factors from different perspectives, it also helps to consolidate the change management culture in the organization.

Define the training and development strategy even superficially. This will provide a preliminary overview of the existing resources and investments to train other stakeholders in the learning management activity, which will happen in the execution phase. Include your preliminary training investment estimate in the project budget.

Activities

- ➤ Define the preliminary training plan.
- ➤ Communicate and implement the preliminary training plan for those involved directly in the project.
- ➤ Involve the training and development department, if there is one.
- ➤ Evaluate the resources available for learning management in the execution phase and estimate the necessary investments.
- ➤ Include training investments in the project budget.
- ➤ Share basic change management principles with the project management team.

3.9. Assess the Predisposition to Changes and Their Impacts

3.9.1. Maturity to Deal with Loss

Changes often bring about loss or at least a perception of loss. Knowing the maturity of both the organization and its stakeholders to deal with what will be changed indicates how challenging it will be to manage the human factors present in the project. The lower the maturity level for dealing with loss, the greater will be the effort required to help the organizational leaders recognize the reason for the change.

The assessment of the maturity to handle losses can be performed for a specific department or for the entire company. How this activity will be addressed depends on each case, the size of the company, the magnitude of the change, and the number of stakeholders affected.

The factors influencing the maturity to handle loss have both an organizational dimension, which affects collective behavior, and an individual one, which has to do with the way each person handles the change. Keeping in mind the influence of these factors on the change scenario will allow for monitoring both the collective effort and the focus on individuals to ensure that the project's strategic objectives are achieved and sustainable.

It is also important to notice that although the team's level of maturity to deal with the change is high, a team member in particular may not have this level of maturity. In this case a specific approach is required, particularly when the individual in question is a leader or influencing agent. Discuss this particular case with the project management team and, if necessary, update the Stakeholder Map.

Organizational Factors Influencing Maturity to Deal with Loss

A number of factors can influence the maturity to deal with loss at the organizational level. These factors are identified and described below.

- ❑ **Company culture.** Companies used to frequent change manage it more easily, as changing becomes part of the organizational DNA. An exception is when change was imposed, not well guided, and traumatic to the workforce. In this case, the opposite effect is produced. If the change will involve different geographical regions, remember that the regional culture will influence the organizational culture, which will require a separate assessment for each region.

- ❑ **Length of time the task or activity has been carried out in the same way.** Time is an indicator of stability. What always worked in the past creates a perception that it should not be changed. Change managers often hear the phrase, "But I have done this for 20 years, and it has always worked. . . ." The best way to deal with statements of this kind is to ask questions that require reflection from the individual making the statement, for example:
  - ○ Is today's world the same as 20 years ago?
  - ○ Do you live today the same way you lived 20 years ago?
  - ○ Do you do the same things and have the same habits?

- ❑ **Organizational resilience.** Organizational leaders who hold their history and tradition in extremely high regard, revering their heroes as models to be followed and holding their beliefs as absolute truths, tend to be less flexible. Change is perceived as deep criticism of the existing situation and not as an opportunity to evolve. It usually takes longer to process the change, and its assimilation requires greater effort. Organizations led by leaders who overvalue a culture of stability in a highly unstable world tend to have a binary view of life—it stays as it is, or it is all different. These leaders fail to realize that change is continuous and necessary so that the organization does not become obsolete and disappear from the market. These leaders will require significant change leadership coaching to increase their resilience. The strong adherence of leaders to current para-digms provides a preliminary assessment of the organizational resilience level. Preparing the organizational leaders to be more resilient to change will boost any organizational transformation: The company will learn to live with frequent change without significant resistance, and the num-ber of simultaneous changes may be increased because people will absorb them faster, generating less impact on productivity. Building organiza-tional resilience is, in itself, a project that will enhance the organizational culture and create a resilient, high-performance company.

❑ **History of previous losses.** Teams that experienced ill-managed loss carry the perception that any change is a threat. The organization's credi-bility takes some time to be solidified, but it can collapse with only one mismanaged event.

Individual Factors Influencing Maturity to Deal with Loss

A number of factors can influence the maturity to deal with loss at the indi-vidual level. These factors are identified and described below.

❑ **The generation to which the individual belongs.** Young people are more open to the challenge of change. In particular, generations Y and Z comprise people who grew up in a world undergoing rapid transition. Change has always been a part of their lives, and, in general, they are less attached to the status quo. Relationships are more superficial and dynamic. On the other hand, there is less loyalty. The risk of a represen-tative of generation Y or Z leaving before the end of a several-month-long change project is high. He or she may get bored with long-term activities and require special attention to maintain energy and enthusiasm.

❑ **Connection with what will change.** Teams or individuals who acknowl-edge "paternity" of what will be changed feel the loss as something almost personal. Change will be perceived as a "child" that will no longer exist. This feeling can be turned into a positive. It is similar to a father who sends his child to study abroad: There will be pain in the change, but also the prospect that the child will have a great opportunity for growth. For people who are highly connected with what will be changed, change management can channel this connection to the positive aspect of the change, creating a suitable way for these people to express their emotions and collaborate in the shaping of the new.

❑ **Personal style.** Human beings constantly seek to maintain control over the situations in their lives in order to keep their stability and remain in their comfort zone. Change affecting situations related to power and status is more difficult for prouder and more self-centered people. People under the false impression that they control the situation tend to resist the new, either because of their technical knowledge or longevity in their position. These same people can be important agents if they find meaning in the change, a space to express their emotions, and participate actively in the transformation of the organization.

❑ **Leadership style.** The way leaders will receive and communicate the change will have a huge impact on the team's engagement. Conservative leaders, who hold on to their technical mastery, tend to perceive loss in their supposed authority and resist more. Their actions can betray their real opinion, even if they deliver a speech about engagement; on the other hand, leaders with high credibility engaged in the change are capable of inspiring their teams and turning perceptions of loss into a belief in opportunities. Their example will be the major influencing agent on the team's level of maturity to deal with the change.

Activities

➤ Assess the maturity to deal with loss at the organizational level, listing evidence that exemplifies this perception.
➤ Discuss and list actions, as well as the people responsible for them, in order to expand the organizational maturity to deal with loss.
➤ Assess the maturity to deal with loss at the individual level, listing evidence that exemplifies this perception and, when necessary, update the stakeholder map.

3.9.2. The Team's Level of Confidence

The team's confidence in their leaders and in the organization is one of the foundations that promotes engagement by the stakeholders. Note that this confidence should be evaluated in a comprehensive way, considering all levels of project leadership, from the sponsor to the team leader. Teams that do not trust their leaders behave with uncertainty, as if they are always suspicious about something.

In addition to the leader's capacity to provide an example and ensure consistency between speech and attitude, the very history of the company or specific area can influence the team's level of confidence. In a project, the level of confidence is generally high, but it can be low in a specific team because of its history or its leader's attitude. Building trust requires time, consistency, and transparency. Weakening confidence is easy and occurs through small events that show contradiction between words and actions by the leader or the organization. Destroying it can be very easy—all it takes is one distressing event.

Activities

> ➢ Large projects should use surveys to assess the team's level of confidence, conducted by the change management or HR team.
> ➢ In small projects, interviews conducted by the change management team are sufficient to reveal the team's level of confidence.
> ➢ In cases where teams show low confidence in their leader, discuss the possibility of replacing the leader. Regaining the team's confidence is an activity that requires a lot of time and is unlikely to be achieved within a project where the rate of stress is continually higher than in most daily activities.

3.10. Identify Alternatives for Knowledge Management

Projects are excellent learning opportunities for individuals and organizations. The learning and accumulated knowledge can be of different types, including:

❑ Project management
❑ In-depth knowledge of business processes and rules
❑ New technologies
❑ Critical factors for the success of a project
❑ Relationships with stakeholders
❑ Change management techniques

No one leaves a project the same as they entered. The question is whether the knowledge acquired during the project will remain tacit, stored in each human being, or will be made explicit and shared.

All tacit knowledge, the internal knowledge of each person that is not shared, is lost over time and weakens the organization. It is necessary to create a knowledge management strategy before starting the project's execution phase. If making knowledge explicit is not planned in advance, it may not take place. Project leaders who leave this activity for a later stage (when stress to meet deadlines and goals reaches higher levels) rarely carry it out and miss an excellent opportunity to promote organizational learning.

If the company already has a knowledge management department, it should be involved as a stakeholder, included in the Stakeholder Map, and have its roles and responsibilities defined.

A manager of each department must be identified and assigned responsibility for keeping alive the technical knowledge (processes, business rules, and operations of the technologies introduced by the project). This manager does not need to master all this knowledge but rather keep it alive through his or her team, that is, avoid having the company rely on the tacit knowledge of a single person, ensure that knowledge will be multiplied all the time, and keep the knowledge base active and updated. This person also works closely with the knowledge management department if one is available in the organization.

If possible, include this responsibility in the job description for the manager and in the other related people management processes, for example, performance evaluation, skills required for the position, variable compensation goals (bonus plans).

Activities

- ➢ Involve the learning and/or knowledge management departments when appropriate.
- ➢ Plan the strategy and tools to make knowledge explicit.
- ➢ Define motivators for the team to make explicit all acquired knowledge.
- ➢ Plan recognition of the team's contributions to the knowledge base.
- ➢ Plan milestones to monitor quantitative and qualitative knowledge base progression.
- ➢ Define knowledge managers at department level and include this activity in the RACI Matrix.
- ➢ Evaluate additional costs for knowledge management and include them in the project budget.
- ➢ Formalize the map of knowledge managers at the department level and, if possible, include this activity in their job description and in the other related people management processes.

3.11. Establish the Change Management Action Plan

There are no organizational changes that should not be structured as projects, nor are there projects that do not generate change.

Change management must be approached as part of the project management discipline. Having an effective change management plan is important for integration with the project plan—the only way it will be possible to maintain a unique approach without segregation between change management and project management, because one cannot do without the other.

The Change Management Strategic Plan is the main product to be developed during the initiation and planning phase of the project, as we will explain in Section 3.13. A key part of the Change Management Strategic Plan is the change management action plan. This plan contains the tactical and operational activities that will be present from the execution to the closing phase of the project as well as in the change sustainability activities of the production phase.

Sustaining the change, which takes place in the production phase (after the project is completed), is often not seen as a project activity. For most project managers and project management officers, project activity ends at the closing phase. However, sustaining the change will require not only the change management team, but also other stakeholders to make any necessary adjustments and solve any issues that are only perceived during the production phase. Take this opportunity to develop the change sustaining strategy and define the resources, budget, processes, and people that will be part of this activity.

As discussed in Section 2.1, the HCMBOK® has a flexible modular structure that must be adapted to each project by selecting the activities and the sequence in which they will be followed. It is worth mentioning that some activities cannot be included in the schedule because they are recurrent and require focus by the change manager. The following activities are included in this group:

- ❑ Managing stress and conflict
- ❑ Managing behavior and motivation
- ❑ Managing unexpected communications
- ❑ Monitoring team spirit
- ❑ Performing targeted interventions to encourage the use of creativity and participatory processes

The change process is slow and gradual and evolves from project planning to postproject consolidation, when the changes must be sustained. Events that recognize the change process should be synchronized with the phases of the project and include celebrations of the small wins in each phase. A program that acknowledges the specific actions that consistently overcome the challenges of the project helps sustain the upbeat mood, especially in long projects.

Some companies often establish specific benefits and bonus plans as part of the recognition of the project team's effort. If this is not a common element in the organizational culture, assess the risk this approach may pose by causing antagonism on the part of stakeholders who are not directly involved in developing the project. If these rewards are not part of the culture, the project team may begin to be seen as an exclusive group with privileges that others do not have.

Those outside the project will have difficulty understanding why they do not enjoy the same benefits. Their desire to have the same privileges can foster the ambition to be part of the project team, and, because they are not, the chance of bitter antagonism is great. Human beings tend to experience a perception of loss in these situations—not having the same benefits the project team has will be perceived as having lost something that, in fact, they never had. In this case, the discomfort with the situation described may be greater than the change itself, and you will have an additional element of complex human behavior to manage.

When benefits and bonus plans are elements already inserted in the organizational culture, consider proposing a benefit that is already within the company's historical parameters and is consistent with the project challenges and risks.

Considering that the action plan extends into the production phase when the change sustaining activities are carried out, the recognition for achievement of goals and indicators of change assimilation can also be planned for the stakeholders affected by the project. Organizations whose culture provides for defining goals for the purpose of granting bonuses and profit sharing can create a specific recognition program for the results achieved by the change, preferably integrating the goals of different stakeholders whose activities have an interdependent relationship.

Plan celebrations for key project milestones. Include the investments in celebrations and team recognition in the project budget. These are part of the project; when they are not included in the budget, they generate later discussions about who should bear the costs.

Continuous encouragement is required to maintain the enthusiasm of the team. Meeting change management milestones is an important component in encouraging a positive mood.

The events and workshops must be planned in advance and communicated to the team. However, the manager's sensitivity must prevail to adjust the planning to the project mood. Plan, but do not cling to the plan—adapt it dynamically.

Activities

> - Select the HCMBOK® activities to be carried out according to the change management approach.
> - Plan the milestones of the change—events and workshops synchronized with the project's schedule of activities.
> - Develop the program to recognize and celebrate the challenges overcome.
> - Develop the strategy to sustain the change.
> - Integrate the change management planning with the project's plan and schedule of activities.

3.12. Plan the Project Kick-Off

The project kick-off is an important milestone, like a green flag for the journey that will follow. Its programming, duration, and investment should be proportional to the importance of the strategic objectives that motivated the project. Some kick-offs require only a few hours of activity in the company itself. Others require several days of exclusive dedication, in which case it is best that they are held away from the organization. Include the planned investment in the project budget.

All participants, including vendors and even some stakeholders who are indirectly affected by the project, should attend the event. Pay attention to the list of participants. Leaving out someone important will be a significant mistake that you may not be able to fix. Use the Stakeholder Map as a reference for selecting the participants. If your map is consistent, there is little chance that you will make a mistake of omission.

Several objectives can be achieved by the project kick-off.

- ❏ Communicate:
  - ○ The view of the organization's future state expected after the change
  - ○ The purpose of the project—WHY the project will be carried out
  - ○ The objective—WHAT will be carried out
  - ○ The planning—HOW the project will be carried out
  - ○ Goals, expectations, and challenges to be met, and challenges to be overcome
  - ○ The project management structure
- ❏ Align roles and responsibilities
- ❏ Integrate people and start creating team spirit
- ❏ Drive the enthusiasm and motivation of the project team and other stakeholders
- ❏ Encourage the use of creativity to break paradigms and create innovations
- ❏ Emphasize factors that can help promote engagement in the strategic objectives of the project and reduce conflict and resistance
- ❏ Reinforce the sponsorship of the organization's leaders
- ❏ Raise the stakeholders' awareness of the need for continuous change as an organization's competitive and longevity strategy

The sponsor should open the event, stating his or her commitment to unconditional support of the changes to ensure their success.

From this event on, it is expected that the project participants begin to build a cooperative team, which should include the vendors. Allowing vendors to express their commitment to the project is good practice meant to integrate them as soon as possible. Vendors not integrated into the project team may be seen by the group of collaborators as "foreign bodies," stimulating the formation of "antibodies" that will interfere with managing the project atmosphere.

Participatory activities will help to obtain each project member's commitment to the challenge to be faced. Moreover, it is time to dispel the myths and face issues such as low credibility and lack of enthusiasm.

The kick-off is an excellent opportunity for the project management team to observe behaviors and the likely level of stakeholder adherence to change. Define in advance the stakeholders who will be the main focus of observation. Prioritize those qualified as "unstable" or "probable resistant stakeholders" (according to the Stakeholder Map), but be sure to have an overview of the others. Plan to conduct a debriefing session of the event, if possible with sponsor attendance, to hear the views of all team members. Update the Stakeholder Map after the debriefing.

A well-planned project kick-off should include, at a minimum:

✓ Presentation by the sponsor including the project purpose, goals, and challenges
✓ Presentation by the vendors stating their commitment with the project objectives
✓ Presentation of the high-level project schedule and its main milestones
✓ Activities to sensitize the stakeholders to the change
✓ A feedback channel for stakeholders to evaluate the kick-off results

Additional Tips for a Successful Project Kick-Off

✓ Plan the kick-off event taking into account the aspects of the organizational culture, such as beliefs and assumptions, ceremonies and rituals, standards and formalities, language and communication symbols, and values.
✓ Whenever possible, define the project identity in a participatory way, including a logo, slogan, name, and motivational phrase; promote a contest; and let people choose their symbols.
✓ Take advantage of this meeting to align all the participants with the project plan.
✓ This is also a good opportunity to align expectations regarding the roles and responsibilities of the major stakeholders. Use the RACI Matrix as a communication tool, and if possible, perform participatory dynamics, discussing the activities, roles, and responsibilities in small groups, to enrich it with the project team's perspective. This will not only produce a more

comprehensive RACI Matrix, it will also increase the participants' perception of belonging to the project.

✓ Define the norms for working together—basic principles that will guide the team's behavior, critical factors for the success of the project, etc.

✓ Encourage the preparation of individual "psychological contracts"—self-addressed letters containing what the individual expects from himself or herself as a project participant and who he or she expects to be at the end of the project. The letter should address personal challenges, commitment-related challenges, and the learning and growth opportunities that the project can provide.

✓ Use a spirited approach to build team spirit and create a participatory and enthusiastic environment.

✓ Promote social interaction. Remember that in certain cases some of the team members do not know each other. Social interaction builds emotional bonds that sustain solidarity during difficult times on the project.

✓ Encourage the proactive role of the project team as agents of change.

✓ Utilize group dynamics that help the team recognize negotiation and conflict management techniques and when to use each one. Use the conflict management macro-activity as a reference to plan this group dynamic.

✓ Apply assessments that help people understand not only their personal style, but also that we are all different from one other. Take the opportunity to cultivate the empathic communication model, that is, one that respects the style of the audience. A good assessment tool to be applied in this case is Dr. Ned Herrmann's Brain Dominance Instrument (*The Creative Brain*, 1989), which can support you to show the different styles that people use to decode a message (analytical, relational, controlling, or experimental thinking). There are other assessments that you can choose, but this one is simple to apply and explain the results.

✓ Hire an external facilitator who specializes in planning and conducting workshops. In major projects, use speakers who are also recognized as experts on the topics to be addressed.

✓ Invite professionals from other companies that have conducted similar projects to share their experience during the kick-off.

✓ Reserve a good time for feedback from the team—a time to listen to people, understand their moods and possible fears, and make sure they have understood the project purpose, goals, and objectives. Resistance often springs from emotions that are not expressed. Creating a space for open discussion, for listening, is one of the best practices to manage change.

✓ Adopt formal feedback techniques, such as an evaluation of the event, but be sure to make an informal assessment with the stakeholders in the days following the event.

Activities

- ➤ Define the plan for the project kick-off—planning, duration, place, and investment.
- ➤ Include the investment in the kick-off in the project budget.
- ➤ List participants using the stakeholder map as a source of information.
- ➤ Prepare the sponsor and the vendors for their interventions.
- ➤ Define the stakeholders whose behavior will be observed by the project management team.
- ➤ Define the feedback process for participants to evaluate the event.
- ➤ Plan for a debriefing session of the event and update the stakeholder map.

3.13. Develop the Change Management Strategic Plan

As you will recall, the Change Management Strategic Plan is the main deliverable to be developed over the course of the initiation and planning phase of the project. In addition to organizing the data collected during this phase of the project and the human factor management strategy to be adopted into a single document, this plan helps reduce abstract aspects, making change management more tangible for the project management team and the top management of the organization.

These professionals understand better information based on data and facts, have a dominant logical (Cartesian) method of thought, and need activities and clearly defined dates to understand the proposed change management approach.

The development of the strategic plan is primarily a compilation of the activities previously completed. When done in a participatory manner with the project management team, development of this plan enhances the perception of belonging and integration. The strategic change management plan should be perceived as an integrated part of the project management plan and not as a separate plan.

To facilitate the understanding and later approval by the project manager and sponsor, collect initial data (elements of organizational culture, a first version of the Stakeholder Map, resistance and engagement factors) and then make periodical revisions with the project management team and the sponsor. With this cooperative development, the final plan will remain aligned with the stakeholders responsible for its approval.

If you identify quick wins as you are developing the plan, propose their immediate implementation. In this way, when the plan is complete, it will already be partially in operation. The credibility of change management activities will be expanded over time. A typical quick win is the communication of the change immediately after holding the working session to align and mobilize the leaders.

Although the project is only in its planning phase, the mobilization around it will have already begun. The workforce will already know about the initiative and probably will be discussing the changes to come. Thus, immediately communicating the vision of the organization's state after the changes, the purpose and objective of the project, and its management structure is a good practice to minimize speculation and avoid a possible negative state of anticipatory grief.

Note that the Change Management Strategic Plan touches on sensitive issues that, if disclosed, could cause embarrassment. The Stakeholder Map is one of the items that should be managed carefully. Treat it with the necessary confidentiality and share it only with the project management team (in some cases, with only part of the team) and the sponsor. A summarized version excluding these more sensitive items can be shared with the project management committee.

The structure of the Change Management Strategic Plan must address, at a minimum, the items listed in Table 3.3.

Every plan is a set of intentions that must be turned into actions so that the expected results are achieved.

Table 3.3. Contents of Change Management Strategic Plan

Sponsorship	Present the project sponsorship structure considering: ❑ Who the sponsor will be and his or her intended schedule for the project ❑ Whether there will be a committee to represent the sponsor ❑ Who will coordinate the committee
Vision	Describe clearly what the change will mean for the organization—how the organization will operate after the implementation of the project. The vision of the future state must be connected with the strategic guidelines and the organization's vision, mission, values, and culture. In general, organizations with a high level of maturity in their strategic planning model already have an established vision for change, but in many cases you will have to review it to facilitate communication.
Purpose and objective	Define the purpose and objective of the project.
Goals and metrics	List the goals and metrics discussed and approved in the working session held to align and mobilize the leaders. Include other metrics identified during this phase of the project.

(Continued on following page)

Table 3.3. Contents of Change Management Strategic Plan (*Cont'd*)

Elements of the organizational culture	Describe the main elements of the organizational culture and their impact on the change. List how these elements can be used to leverage engagement. If they are factors that increase antagonism, identify both the actions to mitigate the antagonism and the people who will be responsible for their implementation.
Maturity to deal with losses	Submit the assessment of the maturity level to deal with loss at the organizational level and measures to work effectively at the current level. Submit the assessment of the maturity level to deal with loss at the individual level and its impact on the Stakeholder Map.
Confidence	List evidence that shows the confidence level of the teams in their leaders. If necessary, suggest a change of project leaders. If the organizational confidence level is low, present actions to eliminate myths that reinforce this perception. Propose adjustments to the behavior of leaders to reduce the impact of this factor on stakeholder engagement.
Antagonism factors/factors of resistance	List the factors that encourage antagonism or resistance, create discomfort, and make the implementation or sustainability of the change more difficult. Describe actions to reduce the impact of these factors on stakeholder engagement. Antagonistic factors can be related to, for example, paradigms, cultural issues, organizational impacts, low maturity to deal with losses, and the stakeholders' level of confidence in the leaders and in the organization.
Engagement factors	List the engagement factors and how they will be used to facilitate implementation and sustainability of the change. Engagement factors can be related to, for example, adequate communication of the benefits brought by the project, explicit sponsorship, high maturity level to deal with losses, credibility of the organization with the workforce, resilient organizational culture duly prepared for the state of continuous change, opportunity for the development of new competences and career progress, recognition and celebration plan.
Stakeholder Map	Present the first version of the Stakeholder Map and discuss actions and who will be responsible for each action in order to increase probable adherence to the change. Identify people who can influence antagonists by acting as mentors.
Map of risk inherent in the human factor	List the risks inherent in the human factors identified during this phase of the project. Upon identification, these risks must be immediately shared and included in the project's Risk Map.

(Continued on following page)

Table 3.3. Contents of Change Management Strategic Plan (*Cont'd*)

Change management approach	Discuss the possible approaches to manage the human factors in the project:
	❑ Will the resistance and likely acceptance of change factors require greater persuasion or will an engagement-seeking approach be adequate?
	❑ Does the organizational culture accept a coercive approach?
	❑ Is there sufficient willingness and maturity to deal with losses?
	❑ Will the organizational impacts preliminarily mapped require some level of imposition of the change?
	❑ What are the long-term effects of a coercive or imposing approach?
	Present scenarios of change management approaches considering the positive and negative effects of each alternative.
Roles and responsibilities	Use the RACI Matrix to list the roles and responsibilities defined for the project team. Make it clear that another matrix will be prepared during the execution phase of the project to be used in the production phase (after the project is implemented). If the matrix is too long, provide an executive summary.
Project management structure	Present the Project Organization Chart, which depicts the project management structure, scope of action and decision making, and roles and responsibilities of each hierarchical level. If necessary, describe any parallel structures, such as councils, as well.
Project team assignment and development plan	List project participants and their type of participation—partial or full time. List the preliminary training needed to prepare the project team to face the challenges ahead. Present the preliminary strategy to manage the other stakeholders' learning.
Identity	If the identity has been defined, present its elements, such as logo, slogan, branding, etc.
Ordinary communication plan	Present the communication plan containing the communications that can be planned, along with channels, procedures, audience, message sender, and frequency. Make it clear that many communications are unplanned and defined as the project progresses.
Physical environment	Present the need for any modifications to the physical environment, investments, and expected benefits. Explain the effect of the physical environment on the team's motivation and integration.

(Continued on following page)

Table 3.3. Contents of Change Management Strategic Plan (*Cont'd*)

Action plan	Present the sequence of tactical and operational change management actions integrated into project planning. Use images, such as a high-level project schedule, with planned activities and due dates. If the project includes a recognition program for the stakeholders, with additional benefits and bonus plan that are not granted to other employees, discuss the risk of this approach inflaming resistance against the project from those people who are not involved. If the organizational culture accepts this kind of recognition for the success of a project, be sure to present a coherent proposal considering the challenges of the project.
Change sustaining strategy	Present the change sustainability strategy and process. List indicators, targets and metrics, as well as a recognition plan, resources, processes, people and teams involved.
Project kick-off	Present the agenda, objectives, and investments planned for the project kick-off.
Quick wins	List the quick-wins that have been identified. List those that have already been implemented and their results.
Budget	List all investments required to carry out the change management actions. These should already have been included in the project budget.

Activities

> Develop the Change Management Strategic Plan in different iterations during the execution of the activities of the planning phase and recurring macro-activities.
> Identify, discuss. and implement quick wins.
> Discuss the preliminary versions of the plan with the project management team and listen to their suggestions if they feel any changes are needed.
> Present and validate preliminary versions of the plan with the project sponsor and steering committee of the project.
> Approve the Change Management Strategic Plan with the project's sponsor and the steering committee.
> Share the summarized and filtered version of the plan, avoiding items (such as the stakeholder map, for example) that can cause embarrassment with the project management committee. Remember that there may be antagonists in the management committee itself.

> **NOTE:** Figure 3.6 lists some elements that can influence the change management budget, which must be integrated into the project budget. Do not hesitate to include others, if you feel it is necessary.

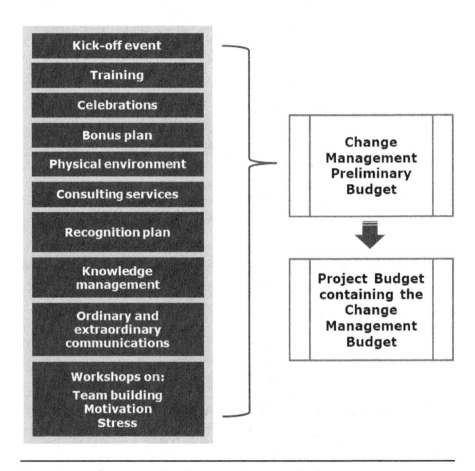

Figure 3.6   Influences on the change management budget.

3.14. Chapter Summary

Organizational change management is a discipline that has tactical and operational aspects, but also requires a strategic vision. In this chapter, we explored the importance of change management be driven through a Change Management Strategic Plan, as well as the need to develop it in a seamless integration with the project management team.

The action plan is also approached in this chapter, reflecting the operational actions of change management. Its main objective is to make the change management operational approach tangible for the project team, with a clear definition of the activities that will be performed, when and how the deliverables will be produced.

In the next chapters, we will see:

- The set of operational macro-activities that will occur up to the production phase (postproject), when the changes will need to be sustained until their institutionalization.
- The recurring macro-activities that go through the entire change process. These macro-activities are the tactical ones, such as: Plan and Manage Communication; Create Team Spirit and Carry Out Reinforcement Dynamics; Encourage Participatory Processes; Manage Conflicts, Motivation, Stress, and Behaviors; Encourage Creativity and Innovation and Manage Stakeholder Engagement.

Chapter 4

Acquisition

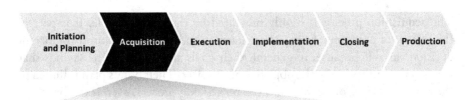

The *acquisition phase* is the period when the project develops actions related to negotiations with vendors. If your change initiative will use only in-house resources, just move to the next chapter.

The acquisition phase often extends for a long period of time; a significant portion may take place in parallel with the execution of the project.

We chose to describe the activities of this phase from the standpoint of *the customer who is acquiring a product, a service, or a business.* There are other types of organizational change, for example, business process reengineering, internal product or service development, even outsourcing. Many of the activities will be the same as those discussed here; however, there may be differences. You will need to determine the applicable activities as part of your planning process.

In the particular case of a business acquisition project, whenever the text mentions "vendors," consider them stakeholders of the acquired company. Remember, after the acquisition there will be a cultural fusion that can affect both the acquired company's stakeholders and those of the buying company. In the case of acquisition of another organization or a merger of two or more entities, consider a comprehensive review of the Stakeholder Map during the acquisition phase.

From the point of view of human factor management, it is from this phase on that new stakeholders come into play—individuals from the vendor side of the project. With a new culture entering the project, managing the human factors is more complex and requires activities that promote integration and harmony of organizational styles. Although they have the same purpose, their objectives may be different from those of the customers—profit is often the vendors' primary objective.

If you are a vendor, take the initiative to include these activities in your negotiation process and project development plan.

4.1. Plan the Human Aspects of the Acquisition Process

The acquisition process is highly pressured by the price variable. It is part of the culture of procurement departments to consider cost as the most important decision variable because, in general, their goals are related to the savings that result and not necessarily the objective of a project. Their bonus plan is linked to the cost reductions obtained from the purchasing process, even if the purchase of those commodities, products, or services is closely related to the achievement of the strategic objectives of the organization's programs and projects.

Our view is that procurement departments should be broken down into two subdivisions—one focused on nonstrategic purchases and another that works on the supporting programs and projects with high impact on the business. The latter should have as an objective the development of sustainable relationships with strategic partners.

In many cases, technical factors are also considered in the final equation that leads to the decision for one vendor over another. However, the organizational culture variable is rarely taken into account.

The acquisition of an automated production line or technology system is not just a purchase; it is the beginning of a long-term strategic relationship with business partners—partners whose replacement in the future will cost much more than a possible price reduction obtained from the negotiation.

In this sense, taking into account the human aspects of an acquisition can make all the difference between the success or failure of a long-term project.

Similar to the vendor's technical features, its organizational culture should also be considered. Making use of a project to develop new elements of organizational culture brought by a vendor is not necessarily a flawed idea. The flaw is omitting this activity from the change plan and letting the cultural differences lead to conflicts that will impact the development of the project and its strategic objectives.

A effective practice to be observed in relevant, long-term projects is to ensure that the business partner has a talent retention strategy as well as a knowledge management strategy.

It is up to your vendor to ensure the quality of service; a good part of this quality will ultimately come from the members of the vendor's team who will be interacting with your organization during the project.

Without a retention plan (which may include career or bonus plans for those who stay until the end of the project), you may lose important members who are part of the vendors' team as the project nears its end. This will affect the quality of the service and, above all, your commitment to deliver the planned changes.

Vendors are also stakeholders, and their people will be affected by the same concerns common to a team entirely dedicated to the project—each person from the vendor's team will be worried about his or her job and his or her position in the company, just like the members of the project team. The imminent completion of the project always brings doubt about the existence of new projects on which the vendor's team can work.

It is up to the change management team to discuss with the procurement department the need to take into account, when selecting vendors, not only technical criteria and price, but also the cultural factors.

Activities

> Structure the vendor's selection process taking cultural impacts into account.
> Ensure that vendors will have a talent retention plan as well as a knowledge management strategy.

4.2. Assess Risks of Cultural Clashes between Vendors and the Team

The process of selecting vendors should already take into account their cultural profile. The lowest cost and best technical profile will not always produce the best results. Especially when the vendor's culture clashes with the customer's, the risk of conflicts that could harm the project climate may lead to delays and unplanned costs. In the end, what seemed to be the least expensive solution may end up being more expensive in every sense—cost and quality among other factors.

For example, vendors in countries such as Canada and Germany are rigorous with regard to planning and will only accept overtime work in exceptional cases. In other countries where people are used to working in excess of planned working hours, this cultural difference may signal low commitment on the part of the vendor. For these countries, their own lack of discipline in meeting schedules generates discomfort in many vendors. This is the perfect setting for a cultural clash.

Cultural differences on both sides need to be identified and discussed between customers and vendors before they give rise to conflicts. If not handled properly, conflicts during periods of increased stress can lead to crises that will harm the progress of the project.

Stimulate a partnering environment, signing a pact of mutual commitment to behavioral adjustments and norms for working together between the internal team and the vendors. Do not allow informal discussions without some form of documentation, so that the harmonization established at this early stage of the project is not lost later on in the project.

Once the vendors are selected, it is important to treat them as part of the project and not as a foreigner in the contracting company.

Activities

- ➤ Assess and understand the vendor's culture. Visit the vendor and pay attention to the company's workplace. Read the bulletin boards to understand the communication style and themes that are part of the agenda of the organization. The physical environment is a good indicator of the organizational culture.
- ➤ Present the characteristics of the contracting party's organizational culture to the vendors.
- ➤ Identify possible areas of conflict.
- ➤ Find points of equilibrium and create mutual commitment to behavioral adjustments between the in-house team and vendors.

4.3. Define the Team's Additional Technical Training Needs

Vendor selection may result in the use of technologies, methodologies, or processes that are not specified in the planning phase. It is necessary to evaluate whether the original training plan is still adequate and to adapt it whenever necessary.

The preparation of the team is an activity that creates not only knowledge but also psychological security and confidence in the future of the project as well as facilitating engagement. Training is one of the most important operational activities of change management. A good practice is to have it as part of the statement of work in the contract and in the RFP (Request for Proposal).

Underestimating this activity may affect the project schedule, as it will be more difficult for the team to carry out defined tasks. It is not uncommon for project managers to realize the need for additional training in later phases when the execution is fully under way, creating discomfort and insecurity among the project team.

Start executing the training plan as soon as possible. It is better to start the execution phase with the team properly prepared than to start training only during subsequent phases of the project. If training will only be provided during future phases of the project, communicate the training plan immediately, to build confidence in the team.

A good training plan has two direct effects on the project. One meets a logical demand for technical skills that will influence team performance and the quality of what is being created. Another is related to psychological security, that is, creating a positive atmosphere among the project participants. It is promoting a perception that the project is an opportunity for career development and that the organization is willing to invest in the future of its employees.

Activities

> Include the training of the project team as part of the statement of work in the contract and in the RFP (Request for Proposal).
> Evaluate whether all project participants have the technical competencies required to develop the activities. Consider the possibility of there being both individual and collective needs.
> Adjust the training plan developed during the project planning phase.
> Communicate the result of the revision of the training plan to the project team.
> Make sure that all stakeholders who are directly involved in the project are comfortable with the final plan.
> Start executing the project team's training plan as soon as possible.

4.4. Map Vendors' Leadership Styles

Even if the vendor's culture has already been mapped, the vendor's performance will depend on the team that will work on the project. In fact, once the vendor agreement is signed, the team assigned to the project, and not the sales team, will work with you.

Understanding the style of the vendor's leaders with whom you will be working in the project environment will be important in order to adjust it to the in-house team's style.

Often, conflicts between customers and vendors arise from underlying differences between the leaders working directly on the project. Almost always, the profile and goals of the sales team are very different from those of the individuals who will be assigned to work on the project.

Integration and rapport between the project leaders are essential for the formation of one united team, without segregation between the vendors' and the customer's internal team.

Different styles are not necessarily a problem. The strength of any complementary characteristics will form a team with more competencies if, despite the differences, the leaders act in tune with each other. The problem is when differences become incompatibilities. Ego clashes, attitudes and behaviors, and differences related to values, if taken to extremes, can derail a relationship. A vendor leader who is kind to you and rude to the team can create embarrassment to the point of contaminating the project with a negative climate.

When differences cannot be overcome, do not hesitate to ask for replacement of the vendor's leaders. It will be much easier to swap individuals from vendors in this phase of the project than after the execution phase has begun.

This dilemma also occurs in reverse, that is, when leaders of the vendors are uncomfortable with the style of their customer peers. Vendors tend to be more adaptable to situations of this kind. However, even if they are willing to adapt their style to that of another, when a vendor's human values are affected, the relationship can become a latent conflict. If you are a member of a vendor's team in this situation, consider the possibility of asking to be transferred to another project before the one you are currently assigned to enters the execution phase.

Activities

- ➢ Promote integration activities with vendors' leaders—listen and assess styles.
- ➢ Discuss your perceptions with the vendors' leaders and talk about your concerns and necessary adjustments.
- ➢ Discuss potential conflicts and alternatives with the project management team and sponsor.

> **Remember:** You are the customer and will have to live with the project result. The vendor is just passing through the company and will proceed to a new project. If you are a vendor, nothing will be more important than your reputation. It is best to leave a project with irreversible human incompatibilities early on than leave a negative story running through the marketplace.

4.5. Validate Roles and Responsibilities (RACI Matrix) with Vendors

Full alignment is important to strengthen team spirit between customer and vendor. The RACI Matrix, which defines roles and responsibilities, is a valuable tool to use.

Moreover, vendors are sometimes experts in running projects. And, on a program, a vendor may be given one of its projects to manage. Listening to them and validating the matrix designed in the previous phase (initiation and planning), may allow you to enhance and adjust it to the project reality. An outside look always adds value to your original plan. The boundaries of performance and expectations of each party will also have been further detailed at the end of this activity, providing the level of detail required by a project that may not be provided by the vendor hiring process.

When you validate the RACI Matrix with the vendor, you may not only improve it but also increase bonds of trust with the vendor. The message is clear: "I trust you and would like to hear your opinion." No doubt this is an important step for those who are entering a new business, and therefore a new interpersonal relationship.

It is worth remembering that the RACI Matrix is a tool designed to align expectations. Any changes to it must be widely and clearly communicated.

Activities

➢ Present and discuss the RACI Matrix with the vendors' leaders.
➢ Make necessary adjustments and communicate them to the stakeholders.

4.6. Plan Vendors' Integration into the Organizational Culture

Vendors who know your organization's culture will be more integrated into, and engaged with, the purpose of the project. Knowing the business is another activity that affects vendors and enables them to better understand the decisions made during the project.

For vendors, knowing their own products and services is not enough. The better they know the characteristics of their customer's market segment, the more competitive their customers will be. Be sure to provide them with this opportunity and encourage them to suggest possible projects to pursue later.

This is an excellent opportunity for creating an integrated team spirit. Vendors will appreciate the time dedicated to their integration into the customer's culture and the opportunity to get to know the market and its peculiarities. Invest time in this activity, as a return is typically guaranteed.

Activities

- ➢ Promote visits of vendors to business areas.
- ➢ Ask the vendors to walk around the company, breathe the rhythm of production, the organizational culture and climate.
- ➢ Present the company's mission, vision, and values.
- ➢ Present the vision of the future state of the organization and purpose, objective, goals, and success metrics of the project.
- ➢ Discuss market and competitive uniqueness and the company's differentiation factors.

Chapter 5

Execution

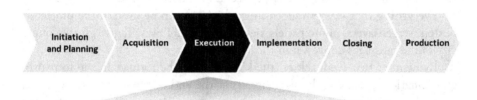

| Initiation and Planning | Acquisition | Execution | Implementation | Closing | Production |

The *execution phase* is usually the longest phase of a project. During this phase, the whole team will be mobilized, and the project will begin to interact with other stakeholders who may have some involvement in the project. Many of them will be directly affected by the changes.

Communication efforts, attention to project climate, motivation, stress, behaviors, conflicts, team spirit, encouraging creativity—all require total focus.

The sooner problems are detected and managed, the better. Issues not resolved in this phase may seriously hurt the project. Their effects will be felt in later phases, when deadlines, cost, and quality may be compromised.

It is essential that this phase starts well with an inspirational Project Kick-off!

5.1. Carry Out the Project Kick-Off Event

The kick-off marks the beginning of project execution. Flowing from the kick-off, all the planning that was done in the previous phases will be put into action.

This activity is essential, as a good start to the execution phase is critical. A large part of the project team will get their first impressions of what is to come from this event.

In large projects, the kick-off should be performed for at least one day, preferably two. If possible, carry out the kick-off event outside the company, in an inspiring place that allows for social interaction afterward. When this event is held out of the office, the opportunity to interact during coffee breaks and lunch allows more time for team integration. For minor projects, the kick-off will require only a few hours of activity at the company site itself.

The format of the kick-off workshop and the mobilization of the stakeholders around it convey a clear message about the relevance of the project for carrying out the organization's strategy.

In the case of virtual teams, connect them through audio or video conference and give them a couple of minutes to introduce themselves, talking about their experience, areas of expertise, expectations, hobbies, etc.

Everything that was produced in the kick-off can be used in the project as posters, screensavers, photo panels, newsletters, etc. This will give greater longevity to the messages conveyed in the kick-off.

Remember that feedback on the kick-off must be formal, in the format of an evaluation completed by participants at the end of the event. However, an informal approach, through frank conversations with participants on the days following the event, is also suitable. Do not be surprised if there is discrepancy between the two assessments. Look for the root cause with the project management team and evaluate the need to define complementary activities to address any items of the kick-off whose objectives were not fully achieved.

It is worth mentioning that the kick-off is an important opportunity to observe the behavior of stakeholders. Many who are uncomfortable with the project will not be able to hide their emotions. In some people, opposition to change shapes the behaviors of emotional disconnection with the event—lack of participation, lack of attention to the presentations, excessive side conversations, and escape through the use of tablets, laptops, and smartphones. This is typical behavior of those who are in a state of "presenteeism"—to resist, consciously or not, the mobilization toward the change.

Activities

➤ Review initial planning of the kick-off and update it when necessary.
➤ Carry out the activities listed in the kick-off planning.
➤ Turn all kick-off deliverables into posters, screensavers, photo panels, sources of information for the corporate newsletter, etc.
➤ Have participants evaluate the event.
➤ Measure the kick-off's success by its capacity to align expectations, integrate and engage the stakeholders, share the vision of future state, objective, goals, purpose of the project, and provide the first step toward building project team spirit without segregation between the different stakeholders involved.
➤ Evaluate the kick-off results with the project management team and plan complementary activities when necessary.

5.2. Assess Organizational Impacts

Expected organizational impacts have already been assessed and listed during the initiation and planning phases of the project. However, there are other impacts that will be detected only during the execution of the project.

During the execution phase, the business blueprint and the details of a new technology, process, or organizational structure will enable the effects of the change to become clearer, especially those that relate directly to the day-to-day operation of the company and its people.

The process for assessing organizational impacts can include a variety of sources, such as interviews, questionnaires, and meetings, to define how the organization will operate in its future state.

Once identified, the impacts must be assessed for their degree of severity. Actions to deal with the impacts must be identified, and the person who will be responsible for executing them appointed.

Many of these impacts may seem less important but will have a direct effect on the results expected from the change, not only on the motivation and engagement of the stakeholders during the project, but also on sustainability of the change post-project.

This assessment activity will reflect directly on the people development plan. Consider not only the team involved directly in the project but also the needs of the stakeholders who will be affected by the changes.

Among the most common and difficult-to-manage organizational impacts is the reassignment of people—for both the project team and the other stakeholders. There may be a reduction in staff, elimination of functions, changes in technical profiles—a series of consequences of the change that, even when treated confidentially, tend to be easily detected by people.

It is also necessary to review the original assignment plan of the post-project team. If change communication is not well managed and the organizational effects change the original reassignment plan of the project team, there is a risk of the team's confidence in their leaders shifting. As a result, the credibility of the change leaders can be significantly affected, jeopardizing the project's objectives and in turn those of the organization.

Project communication planning requires special attention at this phase, when the risk of rumors typically increases. The principles of transparency and increased communication apply here. The greater the stakeholders' level of confidence in the change leaders, the greater will be the credibility of the communication. Everything that is not officially communicated during the change process provides room for speculation and gives a voice to "corporate gossip."

Assessing the volume of related impacts and their degree of severity enables anticipating how, and to what extent, individuals, teams, and the organization will be affected, as well as enabling the following actions:

- ❏ A revision of the Stakeholder Map
- ❏ Issuance of extraordinary (unplanned) communications
- ❏ Actions to reduce the factors of resistance and antagonism
- ❏ Strengthening of the engagement factors
- ❏ Identification of the risks inherent to the human factor

There may be several types of impacts as a result of the changes produced by a project. The following list contains the impacts that most often require assessments:

- ❏ Revision of organizational structures
- ❏ Merging, concentration, or segregation of activities
- ❏ Area or department integration
- ❏ Changes in the level of autonomy of the functions
- ❏ Changes in the status and authority structure of the staff
- ❏ Increased rigor with formalities
- ❏ Staff reduction or increases
- ❏ Adequate functional profiles
- ❏ New management competencies that will be required
- ❏ New technical competencies
- ❏ Implications for other processes or systems
- ❏ Infrastructure implications
- ❏ Behavioral and cultural changes

It is important to note that, even though it is not desirable, it is not uncommon for some impacts to be perceived even later, when the project is already in the production phase.

Activities

> ➤ Compile organizational impacts identified in the planning phase.
> ➤ Assess organizational impacts resulting from what was clarified in the execution phase as a consequence of new technologies, changes in processes, organizational structure, etc.
> ➤ Develop an action plan to handle the organizational impacts.
> ➤ Establish a plan to relocate the stakeholders affected by the project in accordance with the changes to the organizational structure.

5.3. Plan and Execute Learning and Acquired Knowledge Management

In addition to new knowledge, learning management provides security to stakeholders, reducing the impact of the change both logically and psychologically.

If the organization has an established training and development department, it should be involved from the planning phase. If it has not been, consider hiring a specialist provider for this task, as learning is a key success factor in the change process.

Even if there is a training and development department, the department requires significant support from the project to structure the training and development plan with key information that only project personnel can provide. In any case, do not hesitate to get involved in learning management, as this activity is a critical factor in the success of any change.

Training and development needs will become evident throughout this phase of the project. Identify all new knowledge and skills necessary for the success of the change and the target audience for each group of stakeholders who will need training.

❑ Although the project team will have started to develop new knowledge in the planning and acquisition phases, now is the time to revise the plan prepared earlier, adding training in technical and behavioral skills that have not been addressed.
❑ There will be training needs for stakeholders who are not part of the project team, such as systems users and other employees affected by the changes.

❑ Some changes may require new knowledge from stakeholders who are outside the company, such as vendors and customers.

Define the type of training that best fits each audience, considering alternatives such as classroom or online training, self-study, eLearning, and/or use of games (gamification).

Based on this information, project management will be ready to develop the training and development plan for the stakeholders affected by the change and to make a detailed estimate of the required resources and costs.

The training materials should be prepared carefully. In complex projects with extensive new knowledge assets, consider hiring a company that specializes in this type of service.

Some cultures require training to be more active and interactive than others. Implementing a train-the-trainer approach will enable live training (in person or using resources such as video and audio conferencing)—generally a more interactive method. This approach not only gives the organization an advantage by creating a cohort of knowledge agents, it also provides a first source of support to answer questions after the change is implemented.

Select the trainers carefully, as they will be the face of the change for many stakeholders. They need to convey not only knowledge but also enthusiasm for the change—selling the change as necessary. Trainers should not only master the knowledge they are supposed to transmit, they must also have the communication skills necessary for the training to be successful.

Many types of training need to be carried out close to the project implementation date so that knowledge is not lost over time. The ideal scenario is to have all components that will change—new technologies, processes, and business rules—ready before the training starts. However, this is not the most likely or usual situation.

In reality, the first training phases are usually developed when the service or end product to be delivered is not yet fully ready and stable. This is a major challenge for the learning management team, as it may create uncertainty in stakeholders and strengthen pessimism regarding the benefits to be brought by the changes.

In this case, it is critical to make clear that the first wave of training is being held based on a solution that is still under construction, and there will be a significant effort to mobilize learning opportunities based on more stable changes right before the implementation. Having a cohort of trained trainers whose knowledge can be updated as the solution becomes stable will facilitate this mobilization effort.

Any interaction of the project with stakeholders is an opportunity to strengthen the organization's vision of its state after the change, its strategic motivators and the purpose of the project, as well as roles and responsibilities. A good practice is to open the training with a brief message from the sponsor or an organization executive (video, audio or even a slide expressing this information), reinforcing these points to generate a climate of enthusiasm for the opportunity to develop new knowledge and skills.

In addition to effective communication of the training and development plan, learning management requires management of quantitative and qualitative indicators. To manage the evolution of the project planning properly, we need measurements using indicators that are important for enabling any adjustments required in the planning—for example, the percentage of people present in each course, the percentage of people trained by department or area of the organization, an assessment of training quality, the adequacy of workload, and tests to check the actual level of knowledge retention of the people trained.

Collect data formally after the training, but use informal approaches as well. Listen to stakeholders to capture their perception of the effectiveness of each type of training.

Remember that one of the strategies of change resistors is not taking part in the training courses and, at the last minute, claiming that they are not ready for the change. Even worse is when these resistors are leaders who enable the change to be implemented when their teams are not ready. The poor performance after the change will be used as an argument to try to return to the previous situation, that is, their comfort zone.

Learning management demands not only monitoring indicators but also the ability to communicate them. A leader whose team does not attend training as expected, for example, will be naturally pressured by the data.

Have each leader present his or her data in a regular meeting of the project's steering committee. There is no one better than the leader of a business area to show his or her team's dedication to the project. The fact that leaders have to present their indicators will make them monitor the progress of the training closely, so as not to be exposed to a politically delicate situation.

A common mistake is for the change manager to assume responsibility for presenting the status of the training. The change manager should communicate this information to the leaders of each area strongly and transparently, making it clear that they will be responsible for presenting it at a steering committee meeting. Remember: There is no argument against data and facts.

All knowledge acquired before, during, and after the training process should be formally documented and included in a knowledge repository, as it will become an important source not only for implementation of the project, but also for sustaining the change. It is the department manager's responsibility to ensure that knowledge is properly documented, accessible, and managed by a structured process.

This is an excellent time to evaluate the performance of the departmental knowledge management function. Using training evaluation indicators, check whether people were assigned by the managers to act as knowledge management points of contact in their departments, and assess the evolution of this base of knowledge not only from a quantitative but also from a qualitative point of view.

Often the new knowledge needed for operating a new technology or process requires updating the plan for continuous training of the stakeholders. In some cases, even job descriptions and functional profiles may require changing. Be attentive to these needs, and interact with Human Resources to keep these documents updated.

Activities

- ➢ When it exists, keep the organization's training and development area mobilized.
- ➢ Review the project team's training plan.
- ➢ Define the knowledge and competencies required.
- ➢ Define indicators and metrics.
- ➢ Confirm resources and investments required to carry out the training.
- ➢ Select and qualify trainers, and train them as knowledge-positive proponents.
- ➢ Define the training and development plan for other stakeholders.
- ➢ Review the Stakeholder Map to make sure that all stakeholders are included in the training plan.
- ➢ Communicate the training and development plan.
- ➢ Carry out and manage training.
- ➢ Measure results and communicate them to the leaders of each area involved in the project.
- ➢ Prepare presentations with indicators and metrics for the business leaders to show the evolution of the qualifications of their teams in the meetings of the project's steering committee.
- ➢ Make sure that knowledge is formally made explicit by documenting it in a knowledge repository.
- ➢ Evaluate the performance of the knowledge manager in each department.
- ➢ Update job descriptions, continuous training plans. and other people management processes with Human Resources.

5.4. Feed the Project's Risk Map

The Risk Map of any project should also include the human factors. The risks identified should be shared with the management team and included in the project's Risk Map.

Define a mitigation or elimination approach for each risk and the person responsible for being the risk owner.

Feeding the Risk Map is a dynamic activity and should be carried out throughout the project.

Risks related to the human factor can have multiple sources and types, and the project management team should be prepared to identify them, especially in activities that take place without the presence of a change management team.

Activities

> Reassess the risks identified in the planning and acquisition phases.
> List the risks identified in the assessment of the organizational impacts.
> Review the Stakeholder Map and assess the level of adherence to the change.
> Check the list of resistance factors and see whether the measures adopted produced the expected effect.
> Assess the level of stress and motivation of the project team.
> Discuss the incidence of conflicts between stakeholders.
> Select the risks that will be part of the project's Risk Map, and classify them according to their potential impact and likelihood of occurrence.
> Develop risk mitigation or eliminate actions and identify those who will be responsible for being the risk owners.
> Review the Risk Map and the progress of actions planned in the meetings of the project management team.

5.5. Confirm the Stakeholders' Futures in the Post-Project Phase

Projects are excellent opportunities for identifying and developing competencies. Upon completion of the conceptual design and evaluation of the organizational impacts, the necessary functions and profiles will be clearly identified. This is the time for planning "musical chairs."

The sooner people know their future, the better. Doubt causes anxiety, which seriously increases stress and harms the project climate. Time is not in your favor. Once the new organizational design has been defined, it should be communicated as soon as possible.

Some individuals may be promoted, many will be in similar roles, and others may eventually be laid off and need to find other positions. Each group requires a specific approach.

Here is the big dilemma—especially when those who will be laid off are part of the project. In many cases, upon completion of the conceptual design, some people will perceive that their functions will no longer exist, or will change considerably, or will be merged into other functions. In this case, not communicating the future of team members will create doubt and uncertainty. The climate may be affected, internal disputes may arise, and engagement will drop.

Leaving communication of future layoffs for the final phase of the project may prevent some temporary impacts, but it will certainly create distress that will affect the confidence of teams in their leaders, as well as harming the climate throughout the organization. Future projects will inevitably bear the scars of mistrust and uncertainty. People who remain may not trust the organizational leaders.

Depending on the company's culture, establishing a good layoff plan, with benefits, such as extension of the health care plan, outplacement assistance, and rewards for those who stay until the project is over (or even until post-project stabilization), is important and beneficial. Communicating this plan to those still involved in the project's execution phase can be a good alternative.

However, it is not possible to ignore the disadvantages of any previous communication. People react to loss more emotionally than rationally. Previous communication can create some "project zombies"—soulless people, disinterested because they already know that they will have no future in the organization.

In the case of layoffs of people who are outside the project environment, communication can be delayed. However, delaying communication poses a high risk of the message leaking out to these people and to others in the organization. There is no secret when more than one person knows a piece of information. In this case the impact will be greater on the organization than on the project, but the dilemma is not much different from the one previously mentioned.

Organizations have an organic context, and people sympathize with those who lose their jobs. Even dismissals of people who do not participate in the project can directly impact its climate. Be prepared to deal with some "mourning"; losing a job is terrible for those who leave, but also for those who stay. Even if the layoffs are carried out with dignity, it is normal that the team feels the impact of the change. The change manager is responsible for making this inevitable impact as low as possible. This does not go for layoffs of employees only; layoffs of third parties who have been involved with the company for a long period of time often produce the same sense of loss in a team.

People who are high performers during the project are likely to be promoted. Check carefully whether their technical and behavioral profiles are adequate.

Use assessment tools and psychological tests to learn more about the candidates' profiles. High performance in a project does not always mean success in operational, repetitive functions. Recognizing engagement, cooperation, and contribution to the project results will create a sense of justice and benefit future projects. People will tend to see projects as career opportunities, facilitating future engagement and enthusiasm. The culture of merit-based career advancement will be assimilated, strengthening the perception of an organization that promotes professional growth through its process of continuous transformation.

However, it is possible that some people will feel frustrated for not having been promoted. The perception of collaboration, adaptation to a new function and performance is individual. The best way to deal with the intangible aspect of this activity is to ensure a transparent and structured evaluation process and thorough, dynamic feedback throughout the project. This helps manage expectations, reducing the discomfort of those who will remain in the same positions and functions. The change leader must encourage other leaders to maintain a rigorous and immediate feedback routine, without waiting for the annual cycles of performance evaluation to discuss each employee's progress or needs for improvement.

Once again, the change leader must use sensitivity to suggest the right time to communicate organizational movements.

Activities

> Evaluate adjustment of the team's technical and behavioral profiles to their new roles and functions.
> Perform assessments and psychological tests and evaluate adequacy of the technical and behavioral profiles.
> Confirm peoples' relocation with their respective leaders and Human Resources.
> Define a strategy to carry out personnel movements—layoffs and promotions.
> Communicate movements.
> Develop activities to overcome the "mourning" as fast as possible in the case of layoffs.
> Monitor possible frustration of those who will remain in the same functions.
> Intensify project climate management.

5.6. Plan a Gradual Demobilization of the Project Team

Assess the need for retaining the project team after the project is fully implemented and the changes are assimilated. Demobilization should be gradual, to avoid disruptions that may jeopardize change sustainability.

At this point, discuss who will be part of the team that will be responsible for developing the continuous improvements necessary during the production phase to sustain the change. If the project team will not be responsible for continuous improvement, plan how to transfer knowledge to those who will support the production phase.

Communicate the demobilization process as soon as possible. People like to know their options for the future. This knowledge brings confidence as to what will happen to the team after project completion. Uncertainty is an enemy of engagement and motivation.

Remember that, in some cases, vendors are part of the project team. For these people, approaching the end of a project is often a reason for great anxiety, as the vendor may not have new customers to which vendor team members will be assigned, and they may be jobless at the end of the project. Professionals from vendors with greater employability often seek new opportunities even before the project is over, to avoid "off-season" periods in their careers. This possibility is a risk that can affect the project and cause significant losses in terms of knowledge management. That is why, starting in the acquisition phase, it is important to plan vendor demobilization with the same caution and care as other cases.

If a project team member, with an exclusive knowledge, decides to leave the project before the planned date, ensure that there will be a knowledge transfer approach to minimize the impacts of this anticipated demobilization.

Activities

- ➢ Identify the need for retaining key people to ensure change sustainability.
- ➢ Identify influence agents who will have a positive effect on other stakeholders when they return to their regular activities.
- ➢ Plan the gradual team demobilization with the leaders of the areas involved, including company employees and vendors.
- ➢ Communicate the demobilization plan.

5.7. Define Roles and Responsibilities for the Production Phase

This activity has the same objective for defining roles and responsibilities as was done for the project team in earlier phases. The difference is that now the focus is on the roles and responsibilities related to the future state of the organization. Use the Stakeholder Map as one of the sources of information to ensure that all those affected by the change have been included.

Use the RACI Matrix as a tool to ensure that the boundaries of, and expectations for, each department's performance are clearly defined, as well as a clear definition of their function in the organization. A good practice is to develop the RACI Matrix for the production phase during the execution phase, as the processes are detailed and components such as structures and technologies are defined.

Take this opportunity to detail the roles and responsibilities of the stakeholders involved in sustaining the changes up to its institutionalization in the organization.

The RACI Matrix is an alignment, documentation, and communication tool. Do not leave its development to the end of the execution, as if it were a mere formality. The matrix is the result of the project decisions themselves, and when it is developed in a participatory manner, it generates greater engagement of the stakeholders in their new roles and responsibilities.

The clear definition of roles and responsibilities in the execution phase reduces the anxiety of the stakeholders and the possibility of future conflicts.

Communicate the RACI Matrix and share the decisions with Human Resources so that people management processes such as job descriptions, performance evaluation, goals, and bonus plan are updated.

Activities

> List the activities that must be performed by the stakeholders affected by the project.
> Define roles and responsibilities and include them in the RACI Matrix throughout the execution phase of the project.
> Communicate the RACI Matrix widely.
> Share the RACI Matrix with Human Resources.

5.8. Define Indicators to Evaluate Readiness for the Change

A good practice is to define the criteria and indicators for assessing readiness for the change during the execution phase.

Having criteria and indicators makes the decision-making process in relation to implementing the change more rational and tangible, thus helping to reduce the actions of antagonists who express their opinion based only on perceptions, without presenting data and facts. Clear criteria and indicators are a valuable source of quantitative and qualitative information about readiness for the change.

Define the readiness indicators with the project management team and validate them with the sponsor and committees. Consider the following indicators as examples:

- ❑ Goals and metrics established for the project. Some will come from the business plan, such as productivity gains, others from the working session to align and mobilize leaders.
- ❑ Learning management performance indicators.
- ❑ Process stability and technological solutions developed in the project.
- ❑ The project's Risk Map status and contingency planning.
- ❑ The state of engagement according to the Stakeholder Map.
- ❑ Alignment of the leaders with the potential impacts of the transition from the current to the future state.
- ❑ Preparation of the sponsor and other leaders to act as change agents, reinforcing the need for change even in a situation of strong resistance. If the leaders do not act as sellers of change, sustaining it will be much harder.
- ❑ Adequacy of the communication with internal and especially external stakeholders, such as government, customers, vendors, unions, etc.
- ❑ Stakeholders' level of enthusiasm and confidence in the products, services, or results developed by the project.
- ❑ The influence of marketing factors.

Disclosure of criteria and indicators of readiness for change should be part of the Communication Plan. Their communication allows the monitoring of the evolution of the project, both internally and externally.

Activities

- ➢ Define the criteria and indicators to be evaluated in the implementation decision meeting.
- ➢ Validate the criteria and indicators with the sponsor and committees.
- ➢ Create a tool to monitor the indicators and communicate them periodically.
- ➢ Ensure that the process to disclose criteria and indicators is part of the Communication Plan.

Chapter 6

Implementation

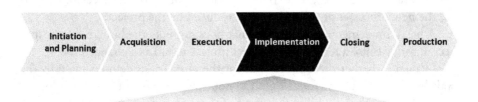

The *implementation phase* is often characterized by peak stress. No project is perfect, and problems, including human problems, come up in this phase.

Additional pressures related to deadlines, costs, and political issues can lead to premature implementation, which can create problems for aspects of the change that are implemented. In this scenario, antagonists get stronger as their criticisms of the new state created by the change begin to have a basis in logic, with data and facts related to the improper functioning of the solution developed by the project. Attempts to return to the previous state are frequent and sometimes necessary so that the business is not affected.

Get ready to manage this phase and decide the right time for implementation based on data-driven indicators of readiness to implement the change.

The stress of this phase can affect team spirit if it is not true and solid. It is easy to watch the project team bog down in a "save yourself if you can" environment—multiple sides can undermine the climate and hamper overcoming the natural difficulties of a change. Assess the need to strengthen cohesion of the team; intensify stress, motivation, and behavior management activities to reduce the natural effects of this phase.

It is in this phase—during which the change affects all stakeholders—that veiled antagonists may appear. Conflict management will deserve special attention to avoid new conflicts or even crises.

6.1. Assess Stakeholders' Readiness and Confidence to Implement the Project

A project, even after all planned activities have been carried out, may not be ready for implementation. Being ready for implementation involves not only the logical but also the psychological aspects of a project. For a change to be sustainable, some stakeholders, even if they participated in training that was successful in terms of quantitative indicators (attendance rate, grades in content understanding tests, etc.), have to be confident that they can successfully operate the new processes or technologies introduced by the project.

A hasty implementation decision that does not take the human factors into account may cause a technically flawless project to fail as a change process.

Evaluate whether there are reasons for the insecurities demonstrated by the stakeholders. Get to the root cause. Do not accept arguments lacking a logical basis. Consider the possibility that some of these uncertainties are actually resistance efforts of veiled antagonists of the change. In some cases, it will be just normal human insecurity due to the imminence of leaving the comfort zone and entering into a new way of working.

Assess and communicate periodically the state of readiness for change together with the project management team, considering the factors described in the macro-activity of Section 5.8. Define indicators to evaluate readiness for the change.

Activities

- ➤ Assess periodically the state of readiness for change, taking into account indicators, goals, and metrics previously defined.
- ➤ Evaluate the team's level of confidence in the solution developed by the project.
- ➤ Make it your practice to listen to the team, understanding that there will be some normal fears about the new processes and technologies introduced by the project.
- ➤ Use feedback channels to hear individual opinions.
- ➤ Address concerns raised by the project team, making adjustments to technological solutions, processes, training, etc., or developing contingency actions.
- ➤ Conduct a survey to measure the enthusiasm and confidence of other stakeholders affected by the change and provide feedback for them, the project team, and committees.
- ➤ Ensure that the stakeholders affected by change took the training as planned and have mastered the new process or technology components.
- ➤ Develop actions to deal with resistance disguised as uncertainty.
- ➤ Evaluate whether possible individual uncertainties are actually representing a larger group.
- ➤ Communicate the state of readiness and create a climate of enthusiasm for the change.

6.2. Ensure All Leaders' Commitment to the Implementation

This is the time to ensure that all involved leaders are committed to implementing the change.

A good strategy is to infuse the implementation decision with the DNA of all involved. Listen to the decision-making stakeholders, some direct and indirect influencing agents (opinion makers), and the sponsor, interviewing them in individual sessions. Eliminate the possibility of some people saying afterward that they disagreed with the implementation for this or that reason, but had no opportunity to express their opinion.

Stakeholders usually have a very busy agenda. Schedule meetings in advance to prevent antagonists from alleging lack of time as an excuse not to express their opinions. If you don't succeed in scheduling these meetings in advance, or someone just does not show up, try to figure out why this has happened.

If you realize that there is no evidence of actual facts that hinder the meeting realization, consider the possibility of facing resistance from this stakeholder in the implementation decision meeting. He or she may be a veiled antagonist stakeholder and may well resist the changes.

Collect information and data that reflect possible concerns or the level of confidence of stakeholders regarding the implementation of the project.

Evaluate with the project management team the logical basis behind these concerns, considering the information and data collected, if any. Discuss alternatives to eliminate them or contingencies to reduce potential impacts. Report to the project management team and the sponsor the general state of readiness shown by the respondents, and then update the Stakeholder Map.

This is the time to discuss with the project management team and the sponsor the strategy to be applied during the implementation decision meeting. The decision on the implementation will be made, considering the readiness for change assessment, and the results gathered in meetings with stakeholders.

Be attentive not only to the speech of the interviewees but also to their body language, which in some cases is more important than what is said or even how it is said.

Pay special attention to the veiled antagonists. This will be their last chance to attack the project and sabotage the impending change.

Activities

➢ Schedule meetings in advance, to ensure that everyone is able to come who needs to be there and then is heard.

➢ Hold a preliminary evaluation meeting with project leaders who are members of the project management committee, steering committee, and any council. This meeting will indicate their attitude toward the decision being made in the implementation decision meeting, allowing you to prepare interventions in advance.

➢ Identify antagonists and any potential barriers lacking logic, and then update the Stakeholder Map.

➢ Coordinate with the project management team measures to deal with concerns that do have a logical basis, discussing alternatives to eliminate them or contingencies to reduce their potential impacts.

➢ Discuss the result of the preliminary evaluation with project management team members and the sponsor, and define the strategy to be applied in the implementation decision meeting.

➢ Prepare a presentation for the implementation decision meeting which contains:

○ The results of the stakeholders' readiness and confidence to implement the change as well as the observations of the preliminary evaluation meeting with decision-making stakeholders;

○ Quantitative indicators and data collected when assessing the readiness for change in the macro-activity of Section 6.1.

6.3. Hold the Implementation Decision Meeting

This activity is a continuation of the previous one. It consists of a meeting with all stakeholders with decision-making power and the project sponsor to decide whether, in view of the circumstances, the change is ready to be implemented.

Prepare the sponsor to be the last to express his or her position. If he or she expresses it in advance, antagonists will claim that they could not express their real opinion because of the sponsor's political pressure.

The project management team must present the state of readiness for change, contingency measures, the Risk Map, project goals and metrics, etc. All aspects of the project must be presented, including the human ones.

After the data compiled by the project management team have been presented, the meeting must be conducted in a participatory manner and everyone must be able to give his or her opinion on the implementation. Do not let unsubstantiated opinions prevail. Challenge the speakers to present justifications based on facts and data. If the preparation for this meeting was successful, the project management team will have answers to all the points raised.

Stakeholders who remain silent should be challenged to express their position, so that the group can see whether there is unanimity or consensus. At this point, many antagonists choose to refrain from voicing their opinion, or may even skip the meeting so that they can say afterward that they did not agree with the implementation. You need to ensure that they attend, and also use the nominal group technique so that they participate.

Define a time for each participant to express his or her opinion. Antagonists can disturb the meeting by expressing an endless sequence of arguments against the implementation. Intervene when necessary so that the time allocated to each participant is respected.

If the state of readiness for change is consistent, start the meeting with stakeholders classified as sellers of change. Leave the antagonists to the end. Their arguments may have lost strength when the time comes for them to express their positions. Close the meeting with the word of the sponsor.

The use of a participatory approach does not turn the project into a democracy. The decision process should be carried out by the steering committee, taking into account the opinion of the decision-making stakeholders. In some cultures, the decision process is concentrated on the CEO or at the highest hierarchical level involved in the decision. Respect the culture but, if possible, discuss with the sponsor the benefits of a decision that involves the steering committee. Ensure that the decision taken is, at the very least, aligned with the majority of the people on the steering committee. Otherwise the risk of increasing resistance is high; there is additional risk in the change having less support than is needed to be sustainable.

Remind participants that, even if there is no unanimous decision, from now on the decision will have to be supported by all. Negative arguments should be restricted only to this meeting and should not be spread across the organization. Have everyone visibly show his or her support for "the cause," strengthening the collective commitment to take the organization to a new state after the implementation of the project.

If the state of readiness points to the postponement of implementation, let the stakeholders who have concrete and logical justifications express their concerns. No one is better equipped to help prevent a hasty implementation than those who will suffer pain from the change. The project management team must be ready to present an action plan to solve the problems that are behind postponing the implementation.

The communication of the decision made during the implementation meeting should list the names of all who took part in the decision-making process in order to extend commitment to the decision made. Close the meeting by defining the strategy to communicate this decision.

Be ready to act as a facilitator in pursuit of the best decision. This will reduce the risk of a hasty implementation for political reasons, or pressure to postpone, motivated by psychological uncertainties and/or opposing forces.

Activities

- ➢ Prepare the sponsor for the meeting.
- ➢ Hold a participatory implementation decision meeting:
  - ○ Present the state of readiness for change, contingency measures, Risk Map, project goals and metrics, etc.;
  - ○ Ask each stakeholder to express his or her opinion, requesting that he or she provide the logic behind this opinion, based on data and facts;
  - ○ Give the sponsor the opportunity to close the meeting.
- ➢ When the decision is to postpone the implementation, present an action plan and set a new date for an implementation decision meeting as well as the strategy to be applied during the new meeting.
- ➢ Mobilize meeting participants so that there is only one message to the organization, even if there is no unanimous decision at the meeting.
- ➢ Define the strategy to communicate the decision made in the meeting.

NOTE: All other technical project evaluation parameters should be available for the implementation decision meeting. Only aspects related to people and meeting the project's strategy were included here.

6.4. Communicate the Result of the Implementation Decision Meeting

The communication of an implementation decision deserves a special section, as the project is nearing completion, but the journey of change will continue.

Communicate the decision to the project team in person and immediately after the meeting. All will be eager to know what the decision was.

If the decision was to postpone, communicate clearly to the project team the reasons for the postponement. Exclude emotions and show that what counts is the committee's decision, even if you do not agree with it. Determine then with the team an action plan with the activities that will be developed to handle the issues and a new date for an implementation decision meeting.

Then communicate the decision to the organization formally and have all stakeholders who attended the meeting publicly listed on the decision, starting with the project sponsor.

Communicate the decision to any other stakeholders formally, using the same format described above. If the decision was positive for the implementation, create a climate of enthusiasm capable of mobilizing all the stakeholders involved in the change.

Activities

- ➢ Communicate the decision to the project team.
- ➢ Create a climate of enthusiasm for the implementation if the decision is positive.
- ➢ If the decision is to postpone the implementation, submit an action plan and a new date for an implementation decision meeting to the sponsor.
- ➢ Formally communicate the decision to the organization and all other stakeholders.

Chapter 7

Closing

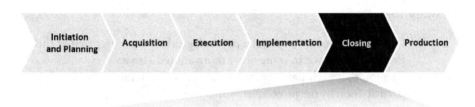

Many career development–related expectations created by the stakeholders directly involved in the project will come to surface during the *closing phase*.

If the expectations are fair and met, the organization will reinforce merit-based career advancement as part of its organizational culture. When expectations are not met, frustration is inevitable and will seriously contaminate the organizational culture, negatively affecting engagement in future projects.

Organizational leaders focused on learning use this phase to consolidate explicit knowledge.

Projects are often politically ended before all the activities have really been carried out, leaving behind a negative legacy and a frustrated project team.

7.1. Execute Gradual Demobilization of the Project Team

Start gradual team demobilization as planned. Turn each personnel movement event into a milestone celebrating the success of the project.

Keep people connected with the changes. If a written psychological contract has been developed in the kick-off or in some other motivational activity, this is the time to return the contract to each participant as part of a closing ritual of his or her participation in the project.

Humans are ritualistic, often expressing their feelings through parietal art (cave painting) since early history. If the organization has a wall that documents the history of its projects, be it physical or digital, encourage people to leave their project message on the wall. It can be a phrase, a word, or an image—something that expresses their participation and strengthens their connection with the changes promoted by the project. For teams spread in different locations, a good solution is to use a digital wall on the intranet so everyone can participate in this activity, leave a mark, and access those of others.

Activities

> - Conduct a ritual to return the psychological contract prepared at the Project Kick-off or in some other motivational activity.
> - Request that each participant leave a mark that represents his or her participation in the project.
> - Execute the team demobilization plan.

7.2. Recognize Team and Individual Performances

One of the factors that encourages a project team's engagement and motivation is the search for self-realization.

Recognition of project performance, systematically encouraged, improves the culture of continually searching for challenges. Participating in a project becomes an honor and an excellent learning, growth, and self-realization opportunity.

Some organizations have a culture of recognizing participation in projects through bonuses or prizes such as trips. Recognition should be aligned with the organizational culture. If recognition involves a monetary investment, the recognition should have been provided for in the project budget.

The fact is that sometimes a picture on the Internet, a word in the organization's newsletter, or the delivery of a certificate by the sponsor is enough to have a significant positive impact on the project team. The recognition is a motivating factor not only for what was achieved so far, but also for generating engagement in future projects.

Let the project team choose the individuals with outstanding performance. If the project management team carries out this activity, some team members may feel frustrated and express these emotions by alleging that the process was unfair.

Activities

> ➤ Promote recognition of the team's work, considering:
>   - ○ Quality of the products, services, or results delivered by the project;
>   - ○ Goals and quantitative and qualitative metrics defined in the macro-activity in Section 3.2.
> ➤ Have the team choose, in a participatory way, outstanding performers, taking into account factors such as:
>   - ○ Cooperation and team spirit;
>   - ○ Enthusiasm and contribution to the positive climate of the project;
>   - ○ Ability to generate results;
>   - ○ Engagement;
>   - ○ Creativity and innovation;
>   - ○ Commitment to the project purpose.

NOTE: Recognize several people as outstanding performers. Consider the possibility of carrying out this recognition event when celebrating the wins and goals achieved.

7.3. Review and Document Lessons Learned

Every project is a great individual, collective, and organizational learning opportunity. Individual learning is tacit and is related to knowledge and skills developed by each person. Collective learning is related to subliminal, unconscious learning and involves interactions between groups, behaviors, change management, and other cultural factors assimilated during the project.

On the other hand, organizational learning does not happen without being orchestrated. It requires an approach that facilitates capturing all individual and collective knowledge, taking it from the tacit to the explicit state.

Organizations that learn how to learn from their experiences develop a strong culture oriented to the continuous transformation of their business.

Innovation is stimulated and facilitated by the explicit knowledge organized in a knowledge repository.

A good practice is to document the lessons learned throughout the project, and then review and compile them during this phase.

The project's close is usually a hectic phase, which often has priorities other than mapping the lessons learned. If you cannot perform this activity now, be sure to do it as soon as possible. This is a way to develop the organization and each participant in the project while preventing future projects from demanding so much from its participants, especially in the final stages.

Activities

- ➤ Encourage continuous documentation of the lessons learned.
- ➤ Hold a meeting to map the lessons learned.
- ➤ Share the lessons that have been made explicit with the project management office.
- ➤ Document the more relevant items in the knowledge repository.

7.4. Ensure Preparation of Users to Train New Collaborators

Even if learning management has been successful, what has been learned may not be fully retained given the dynamism of an organization and the growth opportunities created for the individuals during the project. For this reason, it is important to ensure that users responsible for replicating knowledge are available.

The time is right for you to make sure that the manager responsible for maintaining knowledge gained in each business area remains committed to this task. It is common for knowledge to fade away quietly throughout the company, going unnoticed until it is necessary to solve a problem or meet the training needs of a new collaborator.

Activities

- ➤ Ensure commitment by the knowledge manager at the department level.
- ➤ Ensure that the team of trainers is capable of maintaining knowledge of the processes, business rules, and operation of the new technologies introduced by the project.

7.5. Ensure Preparation of the Maintenance and Support Team in the Post-Project Phase

In very complex projects, critical activities are often carried out by consultants, thereby limiting the capacity of the in-house team to provide continuous support once the project is complete.

Even when the project team develops the knowledge required to provide ongoing support, this team may be assigned to provide support during the project and will not be responsible for that task after the project has ended. In this case, ensure that knowledge has been properly documented and transferred to the maintenance team.

If you have opted for a strategy that uses third parties, the consultant's team that worked on the implementation of the project will probably not be the same team that provides support in the post-project phase. Therefore, you need to capture the consultant's knowledge assets through a debriefing session before their contract is complete.

A successful project ensures the success of the change in the production phase having the necessary knowledge, and, most important, the right people who are well prepared.

Activities

> Make sure that the people who will be responsible for maintaining the technologies introduced by the project are prepared and available in the production phase.
> Develop an ongoing knowledge-sharing plan to prepare the support team.

7.6. Ensure Adequate Reassignment of Project Members

The future of the stakeholders in the post-project phase was defined in the execution phase. In this activity, the change leader should make sure that the project participants were fairly reassigned, preferably as planned.

Avoid a situation where individuals with talent and excellent performance and engagement are treated unfairly after the project is completed.

The organizational distress generated by a failure in this activity may have serious consequences on the team's motivation and engagement, not only in the post-project production phase but in future projects as well.

Expectations created but unmet are a source of great frustration, leaving negativity that affects the confidence in the entire organization and its leaders.

Regaining organizational credibility is always more difficult and tiresome than losing it.

Activities

> ➤ Make sure people were adequately reassigned in the new organizational design.
> ➤ Negotiate possible discrepancies involving Human Resources and the project sponsor, when necessary.

7.7. Celebrate Wins and Goals Achieved

Celebrations are part of the culture of organizations. For projects, celebrating is a change management milestone that closes one cycle and starts another, even if unconsciously for the organization.

This is the time to express one's feelings. Turn hard times into learning. Look ahead and include new perspectives in the organization and everyone's career. A goal was scored, and the players (the stakeholders) need this time of recognition before starting a new journey.

It is worth remembering that the end of the project is not the end of the change journey. Some resistant or pessimistic stakeholders will only begin to be convinced that the change was successful after it is completely assimilated.

Remember that engagement must be maintained in the production phase in order to sustain the changes and prevent veiled antagonists from waking up and trying to reverse the change after the project is completed.

Activities

> ➤ Plan and carry out a vibrant celebration that reflects the level of the achievement.
> ➤ Promote spirited activities, such as drawing prizes, delivering certificates, recognizing outstanding performers, etc.
> ➤ Encourage the project sponsor's participation in the celebration in order to keep up enthusiasm and sustain the change during the production phase.

Chapter 8

Production
(Post-Implementation)

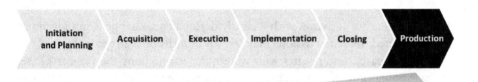

Initiation and Planning   Acquisition   Execution   Implementation   Closing   Production

According to the widely adopted definition, a project is an undertaking with a clearly defined beginning and end. However, if the project motivators are strategic objectives that aim at taking the organization to new markets, higher levels of productivity, profitability, or competitiveness, etc., these objectives can only be measured over time.

Even if the project is successful relative to basic variables such as time, cost, scope, and quality, the vision of the organization's future state will not be realized, and the project will actually have been a failure, if the expected changes are not institutionalized.

Once implemented, the project enters its *production phase*. Note that we are not talking about the period of warranty of a new technology introduced, commonly called supported operation. We are addressing a phase in which the organization is operating with all the changes introduced by the project.

Although theoretically the changes have been implemented, they need to be sustained until they are assimilated and then institutionalized, becoming part of the company's routine and integrating into the organizational culture. No matter the stimulus—merger, acquisition, restructuring, process redesign, launch of new products, implementation of new technologies—the full adoption of a new way of working requires time for the human component to adapt and be in tune with the new state planned for the organization.

This time frame varies from person to person and, depending on his or her circumstances, the individual connection with what has been changed, the level of maturity to deal with losses, and the level of resilience, which means that some individuals may never fully adapt to a new situation.

In this phase, if the project management and sponsorship structure has been demobilized, the focus on assimilating the change is lost, and antagonistic stakeholders may take the opportunity to resist the changes introduced by the project and try to go back to the previous situation.

8.1. Ensure Change Sustainability

While projects are activities with a clearly defined end, change is not always so clearly defined. Its repercussions may last for months or even years.

In some cases, antagonists who were quiet throughout the project phases appear strategically after the change is implemented to attempt going back to the previous situation. In others, organizational impacts not detected during the project appear in the production phase. Your goal is to keep the positive proponents engaged as much as possible, to encourage the antagonists to accept the change and give it a try.

No matter what are the current perceptions, change managers should monitor the post-project period, referred to here as the production phase.

A recurring issue regarding the sustaining of a change is who should carry out sustainability efforts. Assigning the responsibility will depend largely on the maturity of the company in managing its continuous organizational transformation. The state of the art is to have a Change Management Office (CMO) carry out this activity, interacting with Human Resources (HR), Information Technology (IT), Project Management Office (PMO), Process Improvement (PI) or Quality Control (QC), Finance, and the strategy execution team. The RACI Matrix created in the execution phase to align roles and responsibilities in the production phase should include this responsibility.

Sustaining the change should keep the existing project management structure mobilized, even if the configuration differs. If a change manager is the leader of this activity, he or she will occupy the same leading position previously occupied by the project manager. The sponsor, as well as the other agents of change, must continue to be active in this effort.

A successful change project is not a project that simply ends within the deadline, cost, scope, and quality originally planned; it is the one that achieves its strategic objectives and takes the organization from the current to a planned future state. This achievement can only be measured over time.

The time to process a change varies from person to person, so until the change consolidation assimilators are totally stable, change management activities must continue.

Change assimilation indicators can be quantitative or qualitative. The quantitative ones usually have to do with the project objectives, return-on-investment (ROI) analysis, business plan, goals, and metrics. These metrics were identified in the planning phase and improved upon during the project.

The qualitative indicators, in turn, can be explicit or tacit. Explicit indicators are easily noticed, while tacit ones will require techniques and perceptiveness to be discovered. Table 8.1 lists qualitative indicators that can help evaluate change assimilation.

**Table 8.1. Positive and Negative Qualitative
Indicators of Change Assimilation**

Change Assimilation Indicators	Change Inconsistency Indicators
The team's high engagement and enthusiasm with the new situation	Lack of motivation, formal and informal complaints about the problems brought about by the change—a permanent state of mourning is perceived
New productivity metrics	Equal or reduced productivity metrics
Suggestions for continuous enhancement and improvement of the solutions introduced by the project	Attempts to revive old patterns, processes, and tools; creation of alternatives that are, in fact, resistance to the new pattern
A team that is proud and pleased to have taken part in the change	Bitterness and nostalgia; "corporate gossip" spreads chaos
The project becomes part of the professional history of every participant, even those who were only indirectly involved, trying to reap the merits of the project	Participants see themselves as victims, voices not heard during the project; part-time members of the project team insist on making it clear that they did not participate in the project
The project becomes a reference, and the organization begins to focus on new strategic challenges and goes on with its organizational transformation process	The perception that the project was unsuccessful and painful is perpetuated

The change manager must observe the stakeholders' behavior, conduct field and project climate surveys, evoke and openly discuss the issues with leaders in order to identify and differentiate:

❑ Logical issues (simple adjustments in processes that are currently creating discomfort) from psychological ones (an abstract sense of loss and discomfort in certain people)
❑ Specific issues involving an individual or a small group with collective issues

Have a frank discussion to understand the nature of the discomfort and its root cause, and try to eliminate it diplomatically. However, recurring behaviors of the same nature may indicate that the individual or small group did not adapt to the new way of work. In this case, consider relocating people to other areas or laying them off, to avoid jeopardizing the entire change process. The dismissal of only one person having high influence and persuasion within the group often resolves the issue.

An implemented change that continues to create discomfort and resistance among a great number of people or important stakeholders indicates that something was not done correctly in the course of the project. Only the accurate diagnosis of the root cause can resolve the issue.

In this case, the change manager should go through every step of the methodological script—from the original purpose, to the management model, conflict assessment, variations in the level of engagement, mood, and motivation, unmet expectations, and communication. Essentially any and every item that may have left negative effects must have a plan to address it.

Publicly acknowledging possible adjustments needed in the project greatly helps to reverse the situation. Finally, the change manager must identify the limit of his or her responsibilities and, whenever necessary, involve the sponsor in the effort to sustain the change.

An excellent technique that can be used is conducting a workshop to plan the adjustments to be made in the change (continuous improvement). The group will feel that they have a voice, are able to suggest redirections and improvements, find their channel of expression, and, though late, finally engage in the change. In this case, the project management committee is the appropriate forum to decide about prioritizing the necessary adjustments.

Even so, the old saying still holds true: "You cannot make an omelet without breaking eggs." Organizations change, and not everyone can cope with the change. There is always a point where it is worth checking whether the profile of your staff is adequate for the new purpose that has been implemented.

Some people may become obsolete in the organization's new way of working, despite the efforts you have made. And the time comes when the future of these people needs to be defined.

The assimilation of the change is the real marker of achievement of the strategic objectives that motivated the project. Leaving part of the recognition for this milestone is important to encourage engagement until the change has been fully absorbed into the organizational culture.

> **Activities**
>
> ➤ Review and confirm the change assimilation indicators, goals, and metrics to be monitored.
> ➤ Mobilize sponsor and committees toward continuous performance as agents of change.
> ➤ Mobilize resources and people and implement processes to develop activities to sustain the change.
> ➤ Reinforce communication of the changes, its indicators, and goals.
> ➤ Carry out field research, listen to people, and check whether the new process or technology introduced by the project is being fully and satisfactorily used.
> ➤ Carry out a continuous improvement workshop to enhance the change—create a time and space for people to talk about and express their discomfort.
> ➤ Separate logical issues from psychological ones and develop actions to work around them.
> ➤ Define, with the leaders and sponsor, the future of the people who did not adapt to the change.
> ➤ Maintain verification cycles to guarantee change sustainability until the assimilation indicators are stable.
> ➤ Carry out the recognition plan when the changes are assimilated.

Chapter 9

Recurring Activities in All Project Phases

Plan and Manage Communication

Create Team Spirit and Carry Out Reinforcement Dynamics

Encourage Participatory Processes

Manage Conflicts, Motivation, Stress and Behaviors

Encourage Creativity and Innovation

Manage Stakeholder Engagement

This set of activities will be a recurring part of the change project, from the planning and initiation phase to the production phase.

These activities are extremely important in the change management process and, at the same time, are more complex and difficult to manage. Their recurring nature requires attention, as errors will certainly have a strong impact on the human component of the project.

Note that there are significant interdependencies (even a causal relationship) between these activities. Excessive stress can lead to inappropriate behaviors and conflicts that will undermine team spirit or limit creativity. Low motivation of the project team will result in lower stress tolerance. The lack of participatory processes will affect motivation and increase conflicts. Ineffective communication will hinder management of the stakeholders' engagement, can affect motivation, and can lead to conflicts that could be avoided. These are just some examples of the impact that one recurring macro-activity can have on another.

Chapter 10

Plan and Manage Communication

Communication is one of the most relevant and complex activities for the success of a project. Although during the explanation of many HCMBOK® activities, you find recommendations related to communication, we believe that its strategic role requires a specific macro-activity.

The primary objective of communication planning and management is to see that the stakeholders are mobilized, aligned, and connected with the challenges and goals throughout the journey of change.

It is through communication that:

❑ The vision of the change from the current state to the state desired by the organization will be disseminated.
❑ Stakeholders will be involved in the purpose, objective, planning, and execution of their roles and responsibilities.
❑ Project evolution will be monitored.
❑ The goals achieved will be announced.
❑ Feedback channels will be established.
❑ Factors of antagonism or resistance will be reduced.
❑ Engagement in the changes will be increased.

Communication begins in the planning phase and should continue even after the end of the project, to keep the stakeholders connected with sustaining the change.

Remember, there is a big difference between informing and communicating. Informing has to do only with sending a message, while communicating is a two-way street and demands additional effort to gather feedback, process it to make sure it was heard correctly, and assess whether organizational noise has distorted messages.

Good practices require that communication be aligned with the organizational culture. There are cultures where informality is so valued that if you issue a formal communication you may not establish a connection with the target audience, or you may even cause a shock significant enough to distort your message. Other cultures are so formal that an informal contact should not be made before a formal communication has been issued.

Communication has the logical aspect of connecting people with the messages you want to convey, but it also has a tremendous psychological impact that is related to the emotional involvement of each stakeholder with the change. Often, taking time to interact individually and listen to the concerns of a stakeholder who is uncomfortable with the change is enough to alter his or her perception of the facts. For all communication-related activities, creating channels for expression of the stakeholders is fundamental for any change process.

If the organization has an established communication function, involve these people and define their roles and responsibilities. Even if this function exists, the change manager should maintain continuous informal communications with stakeholders, especially because this function often is there for external communications purposes.

Be attentive to any need to involve other areas, for example, Human Resources and Legal. Find out the policies, restrictions, and rules adopted by the organization, and align your communications with them at all times.

10.1. Dimensions of Communication

A number of dimensions should be considered when planning a messaging approach.

❑ **Direct, face-to-face communication.** Face-to-face communication with an individual or a small group is an exercise not only to disseminate information but also to scan for audience reactions. Listening is more important than speaking when using this approach. Face-to-face communication provides relevant information for the understanding of the climate of the project, mood of the parties, their wishes and desires, fears and expectations, engagement and resistance. It is a true thermometer of the project. A face-to-face request is 34 times more successful than an email, according to *Harvard Business Review* (2017). So, walk around the organization talking and especially listening to the stakeholders. Use video conferencing with those who are in different geographic regions.

❑ **Indirect communication.** This dimension offers the advantage of reaching a large number of people at the same time even though they are often geographically dispersed. However, indirect communication tends to be unidirectional and allows fewer opportunities for feedback, making it difficult to understand how the message has been interpreted. The use of a project telephone direct line or contact email, surveys, instant messaging applications, or any other technological resource can be good options to establish feedback channels for indirect communications.

❑ **Individual.** Individual communication requires much more energy and may seem unproductive or not even feasible. However, in many cases, especially for controversial issues or issues that involve antagonistic stakeholders, individual communication can be the best alternative. Encourage the person to interact by asking questions. Observe his or her subliminal signs and bodily reactions. This will allow you to understand how much he or she was positively or negatively affected by the message.

❑ **Mass communication.** Mass communication reaches a greater number of stakeholders simultaneously, but obtaining an understanding of the extent to which the message was properly understood will require additional effort. Interaction tends to be smaller or nonexistent, and you will collect less information about how the message affected the stakeholders. Prepare the entire project management team to observe behaviors when mass face-to-face communications are used.

❑ **Active communication.** Active communications are ones issued directly to a certain audience. When they are active and face to face, such as a project team meeting, proper understanding of the messages can be checked immediately by providing time for group dynamics, direct questions, etc. When they are active but not face to face, such as email, it is necessary to encourage the stakeholders to participate so that feedback is received.

❑ **Passive communication.** Passive communications are those messages posted on some channel, such as intranet, blogs, bulletin boards, etc., that demand initiative from the public to be effective. There are cultures that accept this type of communication well; others will require a lot of encouragement to make it work.

> **NOTE:** The various dimensions of communication can be combined to define a message approach. The word of the sponsor about the project vision, for example, can be communicated face to face to some and online to others who are geographically dispersed and accompany the event by an audio or video conference. In this case, mass communication will be used, but one or another stakeholder may require individual reinforcement of the message to ensure understanding. Audio and video recordings may be posted on the intranet, turning an initially active communication into a passive one.

10.2. Elements for Consideration When Communicating

Table 10.1 lists a number of elements that you should take into consideration when preparing any form of communications during the change project.

Table 10.1. Elements to Be Considered in Preparing Communications

Sender	The one who communicates, "signs" the message, and lends his or her credibility to what is being communicated. An appropriate message from an inappropriate sender will certainly not produce the expected result. If you do not trust the sender, you will not trust the message; you cannot trust the sender if you do not know what the sender believes. The initial communication of the vision, purpose, objective, and goals of a project must be made by the sponsor.
Message	What is communicated. Some messages, such as the presentation template for council and committee meetings, can be predefined. The communication plan must consider the messages that can be planned, for example, the vision of the state to be achieved after the change, the purpose of the project, progress of each phase, goals achieved, etc., as well as periodic messages. It will depend on the change manager's sensitivity to identifying the adequate content for each audience and the time each periodic message will be required. Be careful not to overload the stakeholders with a lot of information in a single message. Customize the content of each message, taking into account the level of detail it requires for the different audiences. A message can be issued initially by one channel and then reinforced in others. The reinforcement provides importance and longevity to the message and can use different styles, such as text, images, and videos, for example.
Audience	The recipient of the message. Typically, a project has different audiences, so messages must be customized accordingly. The main sources for segmenting the audience and customizing the communication are the Stakeholder Map and the RACI Matrix. Based on the Stakeholder Map, it will be possible to define the communication to be delivered on a one-to-one basis and/or delivered face to face.

(Continued on following page)

Table 10.1   Elements to Be Considered in Preparing Communications (*Cont'd.*)

Medium	The channel that will transmit the message. The initial communication of the organization's future state vision, and of the purpose, objective, and goals of a project, should be issued by the sponsor and usually works best if it is active and face to face. Complementary communications can be made using bulletin boards, banners, emails, screensavers, etc. The change manager needs to carefully evaluate the best medium for each audience and message. It is worth emphasizing that incorrect channels can increase distortions of the message. Written communications, especially emails, are usually understood with the emotion of the reader and not of the sender. The organizational culture is an important factor to take into account when deciding the best medium to be used in each circumstance. There are cultures where interpersonal relationships are so important that the mere issuance of email does not produce the desired effect and gives rise to mistaken perceptions that the message is unimportant. The change manager's sensitivity will be fundamental for determining those stakeholders who require additional, direct and individual communication in addition to the other media used to communicate the same message.
Answer	Communication is a two-way street. The change manager should inform participants about the feedback channels to be used for each message he or she sends. These channels must be clear and, whenever possible, part of the message itself. In many cases, listening will be the most important part of communication, as it is possible to infer from feedback the stakeholder's mood, the team's level of stress, the willingness to change, the level of engagement, possible barriers to be overcome, etc. When people express their emotions about the change, they establish a connection with the change, turning a contained negative energy into a state of active participation. The answer has a fundamental, practical function as well. It allows for evaluating whether the communication was contaminated with organizational noise or whether it was clear and effective.

10.3. Types of Project Communication

Communications in a project can be broken down into two types: ordinary (planned) and extraordinary (unplanned).

10.3.1. Ordinary Communications

Ordinary communications require structured planning to identify, through the Stakeholder Map and the RACI Matrix, the individuals or groups who should receive communications at predefined intervals. The plan defines the channels that will be used, the audience, the frequency of the communications, the sender, feedback channels, as well as the medium and message formats that can be established, for example, the project progress report.

The communication plan must be aligned with the organizational culture so that the medium used and the level of formality of each message can be defined correctly.

Usually, the organization already has various channels that can be used in planning. Evaluate and select the ones that are more effective and more suited to the target audience. Also, define communication rituals, such as project team, council, management, and steering committee meetings.

It is worth remembering that communication must be directed not only to those external but also to internal audiences (stakeholders who work directly in the project).

Once prepared, the communication plan should be discussed and validated with the project management team. Estimate the costs involved to develop the ordinary communications plan. Do not forget that there will be demands for extraordinary communications, and the costs of such communications should be estimated as well. Include the total communications investment in the project budget.

Communication, even with a great plan, is a dynamic activity that the change manager will have to monitor and make required adjustments as the project develops.

10.3.2. Extraordinary Communications

Extraordinary (unplanned) communications are based on a specific, unplanned need; sensitivity is needed to determine the right time each one must be used. In certain situations, not saying anything tells people a lot and feeds antagonistic forces with the power to spread rumors.

Silence also communicates in a way that does not allow for managing the impacts of the message. Be aware of what was not communicated by the project management team but is circulating among the stakeholders. In such situations, immediate intervention is required so that the lack of communication does not affect the project environment and create unnecessary conflicts.

10.4. Brain Dominance Styles and Communication Implications

Communication is most effective when it is appropriate to the brain dominance style of its recipient. In spite of controversy among some scholars, for communication purposes, knowledge of brain dominance styles (Ned Herrmann, 1989) can help you define the way a message should be encoded. Taking an empathic position and basing the communication structure on the other party's style is a good practice to ensure that the message is well received and potential organizational noise has been reduced.

Ned Herrmann's theory considers the brain as having not only two halves (left and right), but also two quadrants in each half, with four dominance styles—Analytical and Controlling in the left half, Relational and Experimental in the right half. According to Herrmann, left brain–dominant people are described as analytical, logical, and sequential, while right brain–dominant people are more intuitive and emotional.

Table 10.2 lists some good communication practices that take into account the style of the recipient.

Table 10.2. Communication Styles Based on Dominant Brain Style

Analytical	❑ Develop logical approaches.
	❑ Use facts and data.
	❑ Create graphs, tables, spreadsheets, and time schedules.
	❑ Use expressions such as "analyze," "examine," "determine," etc.
	❑ Avoid:
	  • Long, emotional, or ambiguous interactions
	  • Lack of clarity and vague approaches
	  • Perceptions with no rational basis

Controlling	❑ Show detailed data and items from the planning.
	❑ Present the messages in a logical sequence.
	❑ Use standardized communication elements.
	❑ Establish assumptions and always close with conclusions.
	❑ Avoid:
	  • Delays, lack of planning, and changes in the schedule
	  • Disorganization and breaking patterns
	  • Excessively fast pace and breaks in the sequence

Relational	❑ Show interest in the person, his or her emotions and feelings.
	❑ Show that you are listening carefully.
	❑ Try to find out his or her beliefs and interests.
	❑ Create personal ties and generate a climate of interaction.
	❑ Avoid:
	  • Impersonal, cold, nonenthusiastic approaches
	  • Too many data, graphics, and details
	  • Going straight to the point and pressing for a decision without first establishing an interpersonal relationship

Experimental	❑ Provide a broad and holistic view without too many details.
	❑ Leave room for participation, suggestions, creative and unexpected solutions.
	❑ Ask questions and use expressions such as: suppose, imagine, suggest, etc.
	❑ Listen and create space for possibilities without many restrictions.
	❑ Always present an overview.
	❑ Avoid:
	  • Slow pace and repetition
	  • Too many patterns and details
	  • Limit spontaneity

NOTE: These approaches will be most successful in individual communications, but they can also be used for groups that have the same dominant style, for example, the engineering department of a company. Most engineers naturally tend to have an analytical dominant style.

Activities

➤ Compile data on the assessment of the organizational culture to define level of formality, rituals, existing channels, and more appropriate channels for the project.

➤ Identify the existence of a communications-focused function (internal and external) and mobilize it to participate in the project by defining roles and responsibilities.

➤ Develop an ordinary Communications Plan for the internal and external audiences.

➤ Monitor the need for unplanned communications (extraordinary communications).

➤ Identify types of communication that will be more effective in person; use the Stakeholder Map to assess the need for face-to-face communications, whether individual or mass communications.

➤ Define feedback channels and encourage the different audiences to participate actively in the communication.

➤ Create a positive project environment so that informal communication can be intense, and emotions can be expressed, thus encouraging transparency and assertiveness through the leaders' willingness to listen to their employees.

➤ Observe the brain dominance styles of individuals and groups to determine the best way to encode the message.

➤ Monitor alignment of all communication during the project and make necessary adjustments. Do not leave any misunderstandings unresolved.

Chapter 11

Create Team Spirit and Carry Out Reinforcement Dynamics

If you want to go fast, go alone. If you want to go far, go together.

— African Proverb

A team, by definition, is a group of people who get together to achieve a certain goal. Team spirit is the essence of the work of a group as it promotes a state of belonging and connects people. Ego is the worst enemy for the building of team spirit, because it individualizes and promotes competition rather than cooperation.

The dynamics that encourage the interaction of people around an objective in projects and help build team spirit include the following characteristics and behaviors:

- ❑ Inspiring, consistent, and active leadership through example
- ❑ Willingness to listen, and to reconcile and manage conflicts
- ❑ Clear definition of roles, responsibilities, and expectations
- ❑ Sharing the vision of the organization's future state
- ❑ Creating a purpose that mobilizes people toward the journey that will lead to change
- ❑ Delegation and opportunities for participation
- ❑ Equal treatment and attention to individual needs without granting privileges

❑ Encouragement of social interaction and gestures of goodwill in the workplace
❑ Detachment from and renunciation of individual positions for the sake of a greater good—the staff
❑ Solidarity and companionship without permissiveness and condescension
❑ Confidence in the leaders and other team members
❑ Establishment of goals, recognition and celebration rituals

Projects are usually formed by multidisciplinary teams, often with individuals or teams who have never worked together. By creating team spirit, you ensure that everyone will walk in the same direction, interdependently, in search of the same objective and purpose, as well as everyone's success.

Be aware of rivalries, veiled conflicts, and breaches of trust that can exist between people and departments even before the project begins. These factors will negatively influence the predisposition of some individuals or groups to accept sacrifices for the common good.

Team spirit is a project catalyst in that it uses the strength of complementary skills to overcome challenges requiring a number of different skills to be effective. High-performance teams do not seek consensus, but make their decisions based on common sense. There will be conflicts, but they will be more easily managed by reducing the strength of individual positions.

Recognize teamwork as a relevant factor for the project. Avoid recognizing as examples any individuals who may have negatively influenced team spirit.

People are highly connected with symbols that reinforce their identification with a cause. Teams need an identity that reinforces their sense of belonging to something larger than their individual tasks.

Even if you have succeeded in creating team spirit in a project, be aware of the need to strengthen it dynamically. As the project nears implementation, increasing natural stress boosted by the influence of antagonistic forces and inappropriate behaviors can undermine team spirit.

Teams need leaders. No matter what you say, the team behavior will be based on what you do!

Activities

➢ Make sure that everyone knows and understands the vision of the organization's future state after the change is implemented, as well as the objective, purpose, identity, and goals of the project.
➢ Ensure that everyone knows his or her role and responsibility in the project, and share the RACI Matrix.

(Continued on following page)

Activities (*Continued*)

- ➤ Create events for social relations to appear naturally, as people need time to build respect and companionship. Use spirited activities— a journey, an adventure, games, or anything that is metaphorically related to the project but is not an activity of the project itself. Look for activities that bring people closer together and the success of which depends on everyone's commitment. Do not use approaches that have a winner, as you risk making others feel like losers. If possible, start this activity at the Project Kick-off.
- ➤ Be attentive to conflicting personality styles. Rivalries and dislikes destroy team spirit. If you have no other choice, consider the possibility of redistributing the team in smaller teams of individuals with the same affinities.
- ➤ Do not allow cliques to form, by which people are committed only to their own objectives and begin competing against each other. Ensure that team spirit encompasses the entire project.
- ➤ Identify natural leaders, opinion makers, and influencing agents who will affect the project's environment—they deserve special attention. They can be great allies, but if they position themselves as antagonists, they will contaminate the environment and make everything more difficult.
- ➤ Get rid of the "vultures"—negative people who gripe about everything and look constantly for someone to blame.
- ➤ Discuss the goals with the team and allow its members to help define the challenges. This will ensure everyone's DNA becoming part of the goals, thus increasing commitment. Teams are based on relationships, respect, and cooperation. This is not about creating a democratic, but rather about creating a participatory environment.
- ➤ Look for volunteers to perform certain tasks. You will notice that people who are naturally high performers tend to influence the entire environment with their enthusiasm.
- ➤ Monitor the environment and plan reinforcing dynamics. Encouragement must be continuous to maintain team cohesion.
- ➤ Be open to criticism and suggestions.
- ➤ Be the example! Teams need leaders. If you cannot help solve a technical issue, for example, show solidarity. Be around; buy pizzas, chocolates, and soft drinks. Teams need leaders who stand by them in good and difficult times.
- ➤ Establish **short-term goals** and **celebrate** small wins, sustaining the team's good self-esteem.
- ➤ Remember that team spirit starts to be developed in the planning phase but should be monitored and sustained throughout the project.

Chapter 12

Encourage Participatory Processes

The participatory process is an efficient tactic to accelerate and maintain engagement. This approach can apply to simple activities, such as choosing the name or logo of the project, as well as to important decisions, for example, performance goals or whether to implement or postpone the project.

Participatory decisions require more energy and time from people and can be complex to manage. Select carefully the decisions and activities that will be conducted using participatory processes. Focus especially on those that have the potential to contaminate:

- ❑ The project team
- ❑ The important decisions involving decision-making stakeholders

Be aware of antagonists who insist on excessive participatory processes; it is a way to cause the project not to advance as planned, negatively affecting the time schedule.

Identify those who should be part of a participatory process using the Stakeholder Map. Be very careful here: Leaving out someone who should be on the "guest list" is a resistance-reinforcing factor. This person will feel discredited and disconnected with the change.

When the decision to be made is highly important, make it clear in the invitation that, if the guest cannot attend, he or she should send a representative with decision-making power. Not attending a participatory process that will make a critical decision can be a strategy for resisting. To increase the chances of participation of all stakeholders who should be part of a critical decision, ask the sponsor to send the invitation to the meeting.

From the first version of the action plan, next plan the most important participatory meetings and send invitations as soon as possible to avoid the busy agendas of the decision-making stakeholders preventing them from participating. If necessary, adjust the agenda and resend the invitations after the project time schedule is detailed.

To be useful and feasible, a participatory process must be objective. Long meetings with endless discussions are true traps that undermine the project environment and satisfy the needs of antagonists.

A good participatory process is a process that involves people in the decisions without becoming bureaucratic or affecting productivity.

Prepare participatory meetings using the decision to be made as the basis for the agenda. Allow everyone an opportunity to express his or her opinion. Act as a moderator to manage the more verbose attendees. Ask them to sum up their point objectively.

Before closing the meeting, summarize the conclusions and make sure everyone understands them. Document and communicate the decisions made, emphasizing that the process was participatory, and also document who participated.

Companies and projects are not democracies, nor is the participatory process. The objective is to infuse decisions with the stakeholders' DNA. Seldom will people oppose a decision they themselves helped make.

Making a unilateral decision usually places the decision-making stakeholder in a vulnerable position. People will be able to say that they did not agree with the decision and that they had alternatives to propose but had no chance to do so. In addition, unilateral decisions tend to offend people's egos and generate opponents more easily, often because of emotional reasons.

The participatory process has to be logical and transparent. Often the decision is not unanimous (which is not out of the ordinary), but the decision will have taken into account the different perspectives brought by the stakeholders.

Even if one does not agree fully with a decision, the simple fact of having been involved as a participant in a discussion helps the stakeholder believe that he or she has an active voice in the project and that his or her emotions and opinions can be expressed, expanding his or her connection with the change.

Participatory processes, whether in meetings or workshops, face to face or with virtual teams, are excellent opportunities for the project team and change managers to observe behaviors and the level of acceptance of stakeholders to change. Listen carefully to their individual speeches and positioning. Are they loaded with emotions or based on data, facts, and logical questions? Evaluate whether the comments are positive, or if there is always a negative view of things. Some people express their discomfort with sarcasm or irony; they are often subtle and ambiguous. Focus on body language. Remember that the body speaks and often expresses any lack of congruence between speech and emotion. Take into account each stakeholder's voice tone as compared to his or her natural style. Do not let anyone stay silent, without expressing his or her opinion, because this can be an antagonistic behavior, and you need to gather observations to better assess the position of all stakeholders.

Soon after the participatory process, bring the project team together and conduct a short debriefing session to discuss the behaviors observed. Take the opportunity to update the Stakeholder Map and outline actions that may involve activities such as looking into the root cause of an unexpected behavior and exploring actions to reduce resistance, etc.

Turn the participatory process into a good practice of change and project management. This will help maintain motivation and a positive environment for the change to be successful.

When you feel that a participatory meeting with the decision-making stakeholders runs the risk of slipping into a conflict between antagonistic positions, ask the sponsor to be there. This simple action will put participants on the spot to expose only the logical issues to be resolved, thus reducing, if not fully inhibiting, actions by antagonists.

Activities

- ➤ Identify situations where the participatory process can be used.
- ➤ Identify the stakeholders who need to be involved in the decision; use the Stakeholder Map as a reference to identify those who should be involved in the participatory process.
- ➤ Plan and act as a moderator to make the meeting nonbureaucratic and objective.
- ➤ Observe behaviors and conduct a debriefing session with the project team. Update the Stakeholder Map and outline actions to manage resistance or search for the root cause of unexpected behavior.
- ➤ Involve the sponsor in the participatory process where three is high probability of conflict among decision-making stakeholders. The presence of the sponsor tends to reduce opinions based more on emotion than logic, avoiding actions of antagonists and potential conflicts.

Chapter 13

Manage the Environment—Conflicts, Motivation, Stress, and Behaviors

The management of four elements—conflict, motivation, stress, and behaviors—can be considered managing the project environment.

Projects with a good environment increase people's stress tolerance, keep the team motivated, exhibit a low incidence of inappropriate behavior, and encourage the collaborative resolution of conflicts rather than focusing on positions and individual interests.

13.1. Conflict Management

Conflict is part of human relations and sometimes cannot be avoided. Conflicts are not necessarily a problem. In some cases they can be anticipated and should be managed to maintain a good project environment. Managing conflict is about negotiating solutions.

If managed well, conflicts can often be turned into opportunities for improvement in project management or products and services as well as in people development.

Personal styles, different interests, divergent perspectives and ego clashes are the main causes of conflict. Some activities that help anticipate and prevent potential conflicts are

- ❑ Classification of the stakeholders
- ❑ Assessment of the organizational culture
- ❑ Clear definition of roles and responsibilities
- ❑ Evaluation of the maturity to deal with loss
- ❑ Evaluation of the risk of cultural clashes with vendors
- ❑ Mapping the vendors' leadership styles

It is important to understand the nature of the conflict and separate the logical from the psychological ones. Each type will require a different management approach.

Logical conflicts are related to a different understanding of an issue or solution that must be applied. In these cases, making the facts explicit, using data, benchmarking, and the opinion of experts can be sufficient to resolve the conflict. If the conflict is not resolved, evaluate the possibility that it is a "false logical" conflict, which, in fact, is a psychological conflict masquerading as a logical one. These are antagonistic positions motivated by personal interests or ego clashes.

Psychological conflicts are more complex, can involve personal styles, struggles for power, personal interests, and ego. In these cases, after exhausting the conflict management alternatives, seeking help from Human Resources or the sponsor may be good options. When possible, avoiding conflicts of this nature is the best alternative; this will depend largely on the change manager's sensitivity and perceptiveness. Often the mere presence of the project sponsor in a committee meeting can change undesirable behaviors and help prevent potential conflicts.

A conflict becomes a problem when it becomes a confrontation between two or more people, each of whom focuses on his or her position and turning the situation into a win–lose game. Sometimes the subject under discussion gets lost and winning the confrontation becomes the priority, even when one of the individuals realizes that, from a logical point of view, his or her proposal or solution is not the most appropriate. These situations involve people who handle conflicts through **competition**.

There are also people who, when facing a negotiation to resolve a conflict, give up their positions and do not even start negotiating. This style is called **avoidance**.

In cases where one person gives up his or her goals entirely, the negotiation leads to **accommodation**. The focus is on maintaining the relationship and not defending his or her own ideas.

When two parties have to negotiate a conflict, each giving up part of his or her initial objectives to try to reconcile and resolve the situation, the effect is not win–win. Human perception of loss is always greater than that of gain, and that is how people will shortly, if not immediately, perceive the outcome of the conflict. Managing a conflict resolved this way is basically a lose–lose situation, because each individual has lost part of his or her initial objective. This negotiation style is called **compromise.** Each individual will reach part of his or her objectives and try to maintain a supposedly positive relationship.

Human behavior is complex and sometimes difficult to understand rationally. Imagine that two people earning the same salary ask their boss for a raise. One receives a 50% increase and is happy with his achievement. Shortly after, however, he or she finds out that the other person received a 60% increase. His or her perception will change immediately. Even having received a significant increase, his or her perception of loss will be greater than that of achievement.

We do not mean to imply that giving in and reconciling is something bad or even necessary in a conflict management negotiation. It is important to consider a different solution that can meet the objectives of both parties, thus generating a true sense of mutual achievement and gain.

A good practice for managing an existing conflict is to seek the real interests that are underneath the visible discussion. These interests need to be evaluated and discussed in depth. The root cause of the conflict is what matters, not its superficial appearance. The following examples will clarify these points.

Option 1. Imagine you have only one orange, and two people want it. What would you do to reconcile and meet each of their objectives? Most people respond immediately that they would cut the orange in half and give an equal share to the two people involved in the conflict. What may not be immediately apparent is that the solution meets only half the objective of each person. And there is always the risk that the parties may perceive with greater intensity that lost half orange and not that they won the other half.

Option 2. Now imagine another, less superficial, approach to the same situation—finding out the real interests of both people by asking them why they want the orange. In this hypothetical scenario, when searching for the root cause of the issue, you discover that one person wants the orange to make juice, and the other wants it to make tea with the peel. As you can see, discovering underlying interests—the search for the real interests—can totally change your decision and fully meet the objectives of both parties involved in the conflict. You give the orange peel to one person for tea, and the rest of the orange to the other for juicing. This is the real win–win option, a collaborative attitude that seeks a way for both parties to achieve their objectives. This negotiation style is called **collaboration**. For it to work well, there must be trust between the parties and transparency in the discussion of real interests.

People have natural negotiation styles to deal with conflicts. However, the change manager can moderate the conflict in search of collaboration so that both parties achieve their goals; then the relationship is preserved, because neither party will then have the perception of loss.

Nevertheless, each negotiation in a conflict is a different case. In some cases, choosing the accommodation style can be the best option, especially if you realize that the conflict is not extensive and will not harm the project. In that specific case, be sure to make it clear that one party chose to give something up. By doing so you avoid the other person perceiving that the party who gave something up will act the same way in all negotiations.

In other cases, you may choose to adopt a more aggressive style, such as competition, but be careful to manage the relationship later. In spite of the potential consequences, competing and forcing a conflict solution will often be necessary, especially when there is no time to negotiate and the situation demands an urgent solution.

Finally, when collaboration is not possible, try compromise and then work on preserving the relationship. As we have said, each case is different. Give preference to the solution through collaboration, but remember that it will take more time to solve the conflict, so choose carefully each style to be used for each situation.

Figure 13.1 shows the five conflict resolution styles that can be used as a strategy in conflict situations. One axis focuses on the objective to be achieved, and the other axis on maintaining a good relationship.

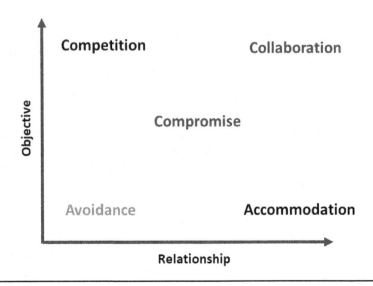

Figure 13.1   Five conflict resolution styles.

Coaching and mentoring are other techniques that can be used in situations where potential conflicts may arise. In general, coaching cannot be used extensively in projects, because this technique requires more time to produce results. Projects that include a separate phase to prepare the team for future changes are an exception. For example, an organization that has decided in its strategic planning process that it will grow through acquisition of other companies should immediately begin to prepare its team, especially team members who have been mapped with conflict negotiation styles that generally incite conflicts.

Mentoring can be more effective than coaching during a project, especially when there is a good trust relationship between the parties, and the mentor has high credibility. A good option is for the mentor to be someone who is outside of the project/change or even from another organization, to better facilitate an atmosphere of trust.

What is most important is that the change manager is attentive and does not ignore conflict situations. Act as a facilitator when managing conflicts. Remind participants in a conflict that ideas should be challenged, not people. Start by listening to the parties separately, letting their emotions flow and practicing active listening. Only then ask questions to understand the root cause of the issue. Evaluate the logical grounds behind the issue and whether the conflict is being completely expressed by everything that is being said. Insist on seeking the root cause—it will not always appear immediately. Try to develop a one-sentence statement that defines the issue and check whether it was understood correctly.

After listening to the parties, propose a meeting to discuss solutions but not to discuss the problem. Introduce the concept of collaborative resolution and encourage a search for solutions that meet the objectives of both parties. Moderate the discussion, trying to isolate emotions and staying focused on finding solutions to the issue. If the meeting does not evolve toward finding solutions, and you realize that the parties are taking personal positions, propose a break so that they can think about what has been discussed. Schedule another meeting and re-assess the situation. If you feel that confrontation is imminent, ask for support from Human Resources or from the sponsor. If the meeting flows well, close it by checking whether everyone understood the solution clearly.

The worst conflict is an unresolved conflict. At some point it will surface, possibly with greater intensity and often as a crisis.

An unresolved conflict can have many causes. One of them is when a person takes a decision based on the belief that his or her own preferences are counter to the group's, so he or she follows the group's decision in spite of his or her own opinion (see Jerry Harvey's *The Abilene Paradox,* 1974). The conflict is still present inside each person in a veiled way and possibly inspiring negative emotions.

Activities

> ➢ Evaluate situations of potential conflict and monitor them.
> ➢ Classify conflicts in accordance with their nature—logical or psychological.
> ➢ Use data, facts, benchmarking. and support from experts to manage logical conflicts.
> ➢ Understand the root cause and the real interests of the parties involved in the conflict, and act as facilitator in the search for a collaborative solution.

13.2. Motivation Management

Simply put, motivation is the internal driver that leads a human being to action. Motivation has two perspectives: one extrinsic and the other intrinsic. Processes of reward and punishment generate extrinsic motivation, while intrinsic motivation is connected to personal needs and reasons.

If we look at the model developed by the humanist psychologist Abraham Maslow (1968), we find five different types of motivational factors or needs:

1. Physiology (breathing, food, water, air, hygiene, sleep, shelter, warmth);
2. Safety (property, family and social stability, personal and financial security, safety of health);
3. Love and belonging (friendship, family, intimacy);
4. Esteem (self-esteem, confidence, achievement, respect for and from others);
5. Self-actualization (morality, creativity, spontaneity, problem solving, lack of prejudice).

The level of motivation of a team directly influences the performance in a project. Using the needs described by Maslow as a guide, the project and/or change manager must be attentive to the effects of the change on his or her team, specifically addressing them in the order of priority shown in Table 13.1. In some instances, in Table 13.1 we have described the needs that are potentially affected by the change project, *using terminology and descriptions that relate to the project and change manager.*

If, on one hand, the presence of these elements promotes and sustains motivation, on the other hand, their absence may negatively affect it. No team that develops a project in the basement or garage of a building, with no privacy and neatness, can feel optimally motivated.

Table 13.1. Needs That Are Potentially Affected by the Change Project

1. Physiological needs	People are happiest and most productive when there is adequate physical work environment—room, desk, chair, rest room, food, etc.
2. Psychological security	Keeping a job is a priority for people. It is important to give the team the perception that the project/change is a career opportunity, not a threat.
3. Relationships	Good interpersonal relationships and emotional partnerships are structural factors. Maintaining the climate of companionship and team spirit helps satisfy this need.
4. Esteem	The sense of achievement and recognition is connected directly to the pride of being part of the project. When the change manager is capable of stimulating this spirit of belonging, he or she gives meaning to this need for esteem and generates trust among the team, thus maintaining high motivation.
5. Self-realization	To reach self-realization, it is necessary to stimulate team creativity; the team must take active participation in the decisions, achieve their individual goals, and see in the project purpose something that makes sense to them.

The factors of physiology, psychological security, relationships, and esteem are essential, and the foundation for self-realization to take place. Absence of any of these factors disrupts the others, generating lack of motivation and, consequently, low engagement with the purpose of the change.

Managing motivation starts at the selection of the project team. It is necessary to find people who are in tune with the project and perceive it as an opportunity to reach esteem and self-realization, thus stimulating intrinsic motivation.

Processes of reinforcement, such as an inspiring physical environment, enthusiasm of the leaders, communication, and purpose complete the picture to create extrinsic motivation. Small wins and goals achieved are also factors of extrinsic motivation that need to be recognized and celebrated to drive intrinsic motivation.

The change manager should consider motivation a critical success factor and be attentive to any event during the course of the project that could change the perspective of the team in relation to motivational factors.

Changes in the initial conditions that favored motivation, inadequate communications, or breach of trust may strongly affect the project team's motivation, jeopardizing the targeted quality and deadline.

Environmental surveys help map team motivation, providing an overall view of the project's environment. To determine individual motivation, talk with people in an informal way and conduct formal interviews, face to face or through virtual channels, but always pay attention to the subliminal signs. Deceptive people can easily report opposite feelings in a formal interview. Creating bonds of trust and channels for listening to people are still the most effective ways to manage individual motivation.

Activities

- ➤ Define the profile of the team that is more likely to be motivated by the participation in the project and select team members based on this criterion.
- ➤ Make sure the foundational factors are met.
- ➤ Ensure that complementary factors, such as an inspiring physical environment, enthusiasm of the leaders, communication, and purpose of the change, are adequate to create extrinsic motivation.
- ➤ To drive intrinsic motivation, identify, reinforce, recognize, and celebrate small wins and goals achieved.
- ➤ Conduct project environmental surveys, observe behaviors, and listen to the team.
- ➤ Promote individual contact with people who show low motivation, to try to understand the root cause of the situation.
- ➤ Carry out formal interviews, paying attention to masking behaviors. Remember that the body speaks and uncovers people's true emotions.
- ➤ Walk around the project facilities; make contact with people, creating emotional bonds and trust with the project team and stakeholders in general. This active approach by the change manager is important not only for managing motivation but also for all other aspects related to the project environment. In the case of virtual teams, prepare someone locally, if possible from Human Resources, to support you in this activity.
- ➤ Carefully observe the mood of each project participant, respecting his or her personal style. An insightful change manager is capable of identifying someone's low motivation simply by looking at him or her.
- ➤ Personally calibrate the environment of the project. Low motivation is often easily spotted.
- ➤ Monitor events that may affect motivation on a continuous basis and apply reversing actions.

13.3. Stress Management

Stress is both a positive and a negative force. Stress is a positive force when it drives the enthusiasm required by the team to overcome challenges—called Eustress (positive stress), a term coined by Hans Selye, a Hungarian endocrinologist, in the late 1930s (Selye, 1955).

However, excessive stress, known as Distress, is a negative force for individuals and is dangerous for the project. It affects motivation because it affects the team's quality of life directly. It frequently leads to a high rate of absenteeism from illnesses such as depression, anxiety, migraine, stomach disorders, and muscle or back problems. In its most striking manifestation, it can lead to *burnout syndrome,* characterized by symptoms such as violent behavior, depression, and physical and mental exhaustion. In this case, people just "go nuts and collapse."

Projects that reach this point need to be reviewed. Absenteeism will be high, and the team, feeling apathetic, will be incapable of delivering the expected results.

Even worse than absenteeism is "presenteeism," that is, a team that takes their bodies to work but leaves their "souls" somewhere else. The team is present, but the pressure is such that its members feel disheartened and produce mechanically, without delivering creative contributions.

Managing stress requires attention from the team and individuals. People can be more or less vulnerable to stress. Moreover, the workload will not always be uniform. It may lead one individual or even part of the team down the path to negative stress.

The rhythm of the project, its goals, the style of the leaders, and the environment are factors that have a strong influence on team stress. If well managed, they can bring about great benefits, promoting team enthusiasm and creative productivity.

Frequent and intense conflicts often have their roots in distress. They can create a vicious cycle where distress and conflicts feed each other, working similarly to cause and effect at the same time.

Figure 13.2 illustrates the level of stress over the course of the project. The natural tendency is that stress increases with the approach of the change implementation. Successful projects see a reduced level of stress after implementation. However, projects implemented prematurely or those that did not produce the expected result keep the level of stress high even after implementation. If this situation continues for a long time, the team's responsiveness will be reduced, and the chance of reversing the situation will be low. Organizational scars leave a negative legacy in the culture, affecting employee engagement in future projects.

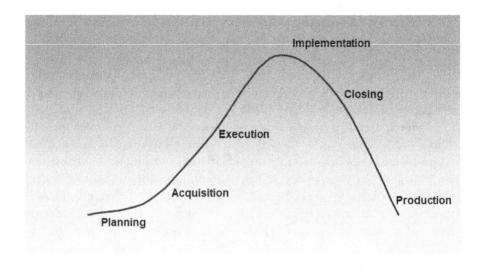

Figure 13.2   The stress curve in a project.

Interestingly, projects that have a slow pace, where decisions are not timely and challenges are nonexistent, also affect the team, particularly the younger Y (Millennials) and Z generations.

A moderating factor of stress, which should be considered in the planning phase, especially in long-term projects, is the vacation plan. Plan and discuss with the team which project periods will be the most appropriate for vacations. Consider factors such as family, children's school vacation, simultaneous vacation of people from the same team, etc., balancing individual needs with project planning.

In our experience as project and change managers, there have been cases where, even before the execution phase, we sent a good part of the project team on vacation. In these cases, the projects were strategic, lasting for more than one year; we wanted the entire team to be highly motivated to start them. We also planned a break in the last two weeks of the year, before the implementation phase.

It is the change manager's responsibility to continually evaluate signs of stress in the team and propose acceleration or deceleration of the activities in specific moments. Using team dynamics and social events such as group celebrations break the routine and balance stress when it is too high.

Activities

> ➤ Observe individual and team moods.
> ➤ Balance moments of acceleration and intense stress with deceleration, celebration, and social events that break the hard routine of more complex projects.
> ➤ Monitor indicators such as absenteeism, presenteeism, excessive conflicts, and hostile behaviors.
> ➤ Plan for vacation periods during long-term projects.
> ➤ Administer the Inventory of Stress Symptoms for Adults (ISSL), a very useful tool for big projects, developed by Marilda Novaes Lipp in 2005. We emphasize that only a psychologist can administer this tool.

13.4. Behavior Management

Individual and team behavior is an indicator of a positive project environment as well as an indicator of problems in the project. Companionship, cooperation, and a willingness to reach common understanding are all factors that indicate a healthy project.

On the other hand, the absence of these elements in individual and collective behavior demonstrates that something is not going well, and the group will probably not behave as a high-performing team. Managing behavior allows the change manager to identify problems and act fast.

Inappropriate or inadequate behaviors can be symptoms of problems related to:

- ❑ Team spirit (or lack of it)
- ❑ Performance of the leaders
- ❑ Excessive stress
- ❑ Subliminal conflicts
- ❑ Clashes of personal styles or different cultures
- ❑ Ineffective communication
- ❑ Project purpose not commonly understood
- ❑ Low engagement
- ❑ Strong influence of antagonists and active resistors on the team or acting individually
- ❑ Little confidence of the team in their leaders or in the organization
- ❑ Fear and uncertainty

Individual and team behavior is dynamic and can vary during the project. The change manager should monitor it continually. It is a primary project health indicator.

Once inadequate behavior is detected, a direct approach through a frank conversation can help understand its root cause. If necessary, ask Human Resources for help to get a more precise diagnosis. Simplified project environment surveys can also be useful.

Techniques such as coaching and mentoring usually help in cases of individuals with problems.

In cases of inadequate behavior from an entire team, the solution almost always has to do with their leaders.

Activities

- ➢ Observe team and individual behavior, paying attention to small signs such as companionship, cooperation, and voluntary willingness to reach a common understanding.
- ➢ Use techniques such as coaching or mentoring and direct approach with people who seem to exhibit inappropriate or inadequate behaviors in order to understand the root cause of such behaviors.
- ➢ Conduct simplified project environment surveys.
- ➢ Go to Human Resources for help to get a more precise diagnosis.
- ➢ Monitor the project environment on a continual basis.

Chapter 14

Encourage Creativity and Innovation

Creativity is like a beard, you will only have it if you let it grow.

— Voltaire

According to research carried out by George Land and Beth Jarman in *Breakpoint and Beyond: Mastering the Future Today* (1998), while 98% of children up to five years old can be considered highly creative, only 2% of adults over 25 years old achieve this classification. As all of us were once children, meaning that no one stops being creative. People just stick to standards and stop using their creativity. That is why it is important to manage creativity, providing the type of encouragement that will enable the team to use all of their creative potential throughout the change project.

While creativity is the human competency to conceive new things, innovation requires an entrepreneurial spirit to select and turn creative ideas into true innovations, capable of creating competitive differentiators that lead to productivity gains and profitability. Not everything that is creative becomes an innovation, but every innovation has its roots in creativity.

Projects are excellent opportunities for organizations to innovate. However, innovations are not spontaneous. They need to be stimulated and encouraged in the organizational culture.

Innovation means breaking paradigms and old habits. Usually, without adequate stimulation, people tend to maintain the status quo. This phenomenon occurs mainly in organizations with a conservative culture, imposed changes, or when the team shows low maturity to deal with loss. In these cases, innovations are seen as threats even though they can mean great opportunities.

It is not easy to get people out of their comfort zone and implement a creativity- and innovation-oriented culture, but the effects are so positive for change that every effort is worth it.

However, the most common scenario is the attachment to paradigms, which ends up turning projects that should produce great benefits to the business into mere technological development, wasting the opportunity to rethink business processes and rules to produce innovations and position the organization at a new competitive level.

The power of the paradigm is such that no means of printed communication, such as newspapers and magazines, could find solutions for the opportunities provided by digital advertising. On the contrary, they were victims of the fast digitalizing of the world. In a decade, these media saw their advertising revenue (with adjusted inflation) plummet to a lower level than that recorded in 1950, according to the Newspaper Association of America (now the News Media Alliance), as reported in 2013.

Similarly, it was not the major hotel chains that created the famous lodging website AIRBNB. AIRBNB currently exists in more than 190 countries; its market value in 2016 was US$30 billion (Huet & Newcomer, 2016), exceeding that of some giant hotel chains, without even having a single hotel.

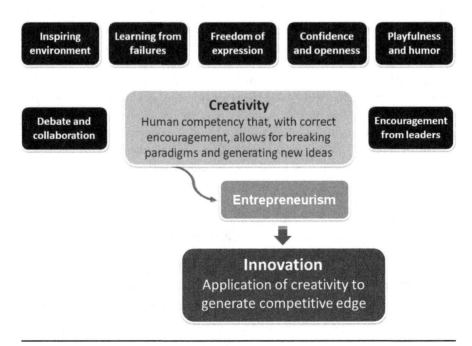

Figure 14.1   The application of creativity to generate innovation.

Encouraging people to use their creativity can infuse the solutions brought by the project with the DNA of these stakeholders, tremendously expanding their perception of "parenthood" for the generated change. The effect on the engagement of those who co-create is impressive. Motivation is expanded and people feel valued, reaching a higher level of personal fulfillment, becoming sellers of change. Figure 14.1 provides a graphic representation of the aspects of a creative environment that lead to innovation:

❑ Freedom and confidence for people to express their ideas without being criticized and ridiculed
❑ Playfulness and good humor
❑ Incentives and inspiration from leaders
❑ Capacity to take risks and tolerate well-intended attempts and failures
❑ Application of techniques and processes to stimulate creative debate
❑ An inspiring environment
❑ Collaboration and enrichment of ideas

It is the change manager's responsibility to aggressively apply and promote techniques that encourage identifying creative solutions for project and business problems, by influencing leaders and acting as a facilitator so that the proper techniques can be applied.

Another way to think about the creative process is to look at a phased model. According to Bertrand Russell (1956, 1992), the creative process has four phases that must be followed to achieve the full creative potential of teams. Table 14.1 lists the four phases together with a description of each phase.

Table 14.1. Phases in the Creative Process (Bertrand Russell, 1956, 1992)

Preparation	Study, read, discuss, collect, scribble, and cultivate the imagination
Incubation	Rest and disconnect from the problem. The unconscious, unencumbered by the intellect, begins to elaborate on the unexpected connections that constitute the essence of creation. The change manager or facilitator should be attentive to the right time to intervene in a meeting to find solutions, closing it temporarily so people have time to "daydream." When resuming the meeting on another day, unexpected creative solutions may be ready to emerge.
Illumination	Here the idea, the solution, comes up. It is the time for Archimedes' classic "Eureka." Also known as *insight*, it usually occurs when the brain is free, perhaps carrying out mechanical activities such as bathing, shaving, or driving.
Verification	This is the return to consciousness, rationality. The intellect begins to finish the work the imagination started. This is the time to test the idea, submit it to criticisms and judgments.

Before presenting the techniques to manage creativity, we will look at two types of thinking that will be used in the process to generate creative solutions—divergent and convergent thinking.

> **Divergent thinking**
  Divergent thinking is a wide and unrestricted way of thinking without any concern for reality. Divergent thinking is literally a no-man's land, without logic, limits, or rules. Anything goes; anything is possible. The basic rules of divergent thinking are
  ❑ Quantity leads to quality.
  ❑ Postpone judgment and encourage dreaming.
  ❑ Do not hold onto or dispose of anything.
  ❑ Explore the unexpected and unusual.
  ❑ Improve other ideas; let one idea create others.

> **Convergent thinking**
  Convergent thinking is always applied after the divergent thinking stage. It involves evaluation, judgment, and decision making. The risk here is that the attachment to paradigms limits choices and takes away from the ingenuity of the divergent thinking. Some basic rules of convergent thinking are
  ❑ Be positive, ask yourself, "Why not?"
  ❑ Be prudent—avoid hasty decisions that can rule out a good idea that at first seems unfeasible.
  ❑ Focus on the original objective.
  ❑ Explore the unexpected and unusual.
  ❑ Improve ideas.
  ❑ Consider novelty; be brave!

14.1. Techniques for Generating Creative Solutions

There are several techniques that can be useful to generate creative solutions, including brainstorming, brainwriting, and SCAMPER (Substitute, Combine, Adapt, Modify, Put to another use, Eliminate, Reorganize). However, before generating ideas, it is necessary to clearly define the problem to be solved.

14.1.1. Defining the Problem to be Solved

The real problem to be solved is often not evident. What we feel as a problem is, in general, the effect of a situation.

In the 1940s, the shipping industry was facing a serious crisis. Cargo transportation costs were growing, and it took too long for goods to reach their destination. Large investments were made to develop faster ships and to lower costs of the crew and fuel, but the result was unsatisfactory.

The problem, in fact, was not in the ship's travel time, but in the time the ship waited before being loaded. A ship is a large capital investment, and the longer it sits idle in port, the worse is its productivity. Moreover, excess time that the goods to be loaded sit at the port means greater risk of loss and theft, increasing the cost of sea cargo insurance.

At that time, a young truck driver, watching the slow loading of bales of cotton at the Port of New York, had the idea to store the goods in large steel containers that could be organized for loading even before the ship docked, tremendously reducing the time of loading and unloading. This idea led to creating shipping containers, which revolutionized the shipping industry.

The perceived effect attributed reductions in costs to improved efficiency of sea transport. However, the problem was not the travel time of a ship, but its idle time in port.

The first step in finding a solution to a problem is comprehensively assessing all of the factors involved, collecting as much data as possible, then gathering a multidisciplinary team to discuss the problem and articulate a statement that clearly and objectively describes it.

14.1.2. Generating Ideas

The second step in the process is using specific techniques to generate ideas. Once the real problem is identified, bring together people with different profiles from different business areas, to work together to find solutions. Diversity helps significantly because it provides different perspectives for generating creative ideas without the usual attachment to installed paradigms.

To generate ideas, use techniques that stimulate divergent thinking.

Brainstorming consists of using divergent thinking to generate the largest possible number of ideas without any prejudgment about their viability. It is a free exercise that should be facilitated so that no filter or critical stance will inhibit the full involvement of people in generating ideas. A basic rule at this stage is to allow for daydreaming and not to discard any idea.

Start by introducing the sentence that defines the nature and characteristics of the problem on a flip chart or that leaves the definition of the problem visible to all. Each idea generated should be written on the flip chart and shared with everyone. After every 10 or 15 ideas, reassess whether the focus on the problem has been lost. An idea can inspire another, an addition of something, or a change to the original idea. In these cases, do not change the original idea. Add your derivative ideas to the list of original ideas. **Remember, this is the time to generate ideas, not discuss them.**

Brainstorming with Post-its® is an evolution of brainstorming that makes the process more participative and dynamic. The fundamentals are the same as those of brainstorming; the only difference lies in the application tool. If a participant has an idea while brainstorming with Post-its during the divergent thinking phase, he or she must write it down, read it aloud to the group, and then post it on the wall. In the convergent thinking phase, grouping ideas becomes easier thanks to the mobility with which the Post-its can be handled.

Brainwriting is also a derivation of brainstorming, and is extremely useful in groups with very active participants that end up overshadowing and inhibiting balanced participation. With this technique, in the divergent thinking phase all participants are encouraged to write three ideas on a sheet of paper and exchange it with the group. When receiving the sheet, the participant must read it and either add something to an idea created by another participant or add one or more other ideas. One of these actions or the sum of the two actions must provide three new ideas. This phase will be over when all participants have gone through the sheets of all other participants. This approach is similar to the nominal group technique (NGT), originally developed by Andre Delbecq and Andrew H. Van de Ven (1975).

NOTE: Encourage as many ideas as possible. The best ideas will probably be a combination or improvement of several others and will be selected from the last third of the total ideas generated.

SCAMPER is an "interrogation" process in which questions are used to enrich the way alternative ideas are seen. This process can be applied together with the previous techniques. The SCAMPER process looks for solutions by asking a number of specific questions about the proposed ideas related to each of the following concepts:

> **S**ubstitute
> **C**ombine
> **A**dapt
> **M**odify

> **P**ut to another use
> **E**liminate
> **R**eorganize

14.1.3. Grouping, Selection, and Enhancing

After the stage of generating ideas based on divergent thinking, it is time to structure them and start to define the chart of applicable solutions using convergent thinking.

Start by asking the team that generated the ideas to group them by affinity and similarity. If necessary, rewrite the ideas to make them more understandable.

Ask the team to select those that seem most appropriate. Create sets of ideas classified as priority one and priority two. Question the choices and especially the motivating factors that led some ideas to be discarded. Use the SCAMPER

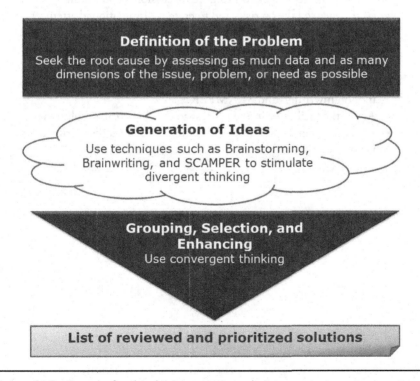

Figure 14.2   Process for developing creative solutions.

(Text describing Figure 14.2 can be found on the following page.)

questioning process to improve discarded ideas, where applicable. Do not dismiss any idea. Even those that are not used immediately may be discussed again later. Store them in a bank of ideas for every problem and even put them in the knowledge repository so they are not lost.

Review the selected sets of ideas and enhance them when necessary, rewriting them as potential solutions to the problem.

Figure 14.2 summarizes the process for developing creative solutions.

If you recall Russell's four phases, the change manager needs to be aware of the need to intervene in some cases and allow participants involved in developing creative solutions an incubation period of one or two days.

Activities

> Create an inspiring environment.
> Develop a project environment of trust to encourage the team to create and provide suggestions.
> Encourage the leaders to promote discussions, good humor, and the confidence to take on risks and tolerate well-intentioned attempts and failures.
> Encourage the use of Russell's four phases—preparation, respect incubation time, illumination, and verification.
> Prepare the team and leaders to apply techniques such as brainstorming, brainwriting, and SCAMPER.
> Act as the facilitator in the process to develop creative solutions.
> Encourage participation, collaboration, and collective enrichment of ideas.

Chapter 15

Manage Stakeholder Engagement

The main focus of stakeholder engagement management is to reduce resistance and promote engagement in the change so that the strategic objectives that motivated the investment are achieved. There is no successful project without a suitable level of engagement in the change.

The process for engaging stakeholders in the vision of the organization's future state begins with a clear and direct communication from the sponsor. Sponsorship is one of the most important elements for a successful change. Having co-sponsors from the organization's top management and entire leadership chain is also a factor that directly influences the outcome of the project.

The ideal scenario is to achieve 100% engagement. However, this is a utopia even for cases where there are no apparent possibilities of resistance.

In April 2015, Dan Price, the young founder and CEO of the credit card payment processing company Gravity Payments, announced a surprising change—reduction of his own salary and payment of a $70,000 minimum annual salary to his employees. Dan Price's decision was inspired by research that shows that this is the minimum amount that people in the United States need to be happy.

In fact, many were happy with this decision, especially those who earned less than this amount. However, negative effects also occurred.

People who had worked years to get to their current salary felt devalued, as any new employee of the company would start out earning the same salary. Others felt exposed because they began to be pressured by family and friends with requests for loans. Two of Price's most valued executives left the company because they believed that the new salary policy was unfair. New customers were attracted by the publicity generated by the repercussions of the case, but some long-term customers ended their relationship with the company, fearing an increase in costs.

Human behavior is very complex; it is not logic alone that defines our attitudes and impulses. On the contrary, we have a psychological side (often little known even to ourselves) that prevails in many situations. It is only with considerable thought and self-knowledge that we can understand this psychological side. Our perception of loss occurs before we realize the gains that will come with the change.

The Stakeholder Map is the main tool for this macro-activity. This map clearly and objectively shows the level of engagement of the stakeholders, thereby enabling the planning and development of actions to deal with antagonists.

In very large, high-impact projects, monitoring a long list of stakeholders may not be feasible. Make the stakeholders with greater influence on the project a priority. In such cases, you can use a 20/80 approach and have someone of the project management team responsible or actively monitoring the top 20%—with less frequent monitoring of the remaining 80%.

Early in the project, asses the expectations of key stakeholders in individual or small group meetings. In the project execution phase, evaluate how much these expectations will be met and provide feedback to ensure the key stakeholders' expectations alignment with the project outcome.

The change manager needs to understand the root cause of resistance and be able to have empathy. Understanding the situation and the effects of the change from the point of view of the other is critical to do so.

In many cases, you will reach the conclusion that a person's fear is totally unfounded. Remember, though, that it is unfounded to you, not to him or her. Every human being is unique and brings into his or her current behavior not only natural and inborn styles but also the effects of past events that are part of his or her life story.

Develop a trusting relationship. Talk frankly and openly with the stakeholders to really understand the sources of their distress. Speak little and listen a lot. The ability to be a good listener actually is not an easy task. You have to develop an empathic attitude and keep your mind open with a nonjudgmental approach. In fact, you might have been trained to be a good speaker, but you probably were never trained to be a good listener. We will discuss more about this subject in Chapter 17, "Essential Competencies for Change Leaders."

Often a hidden part of the situation will not be articulated. Use your skill to find what lies beneath appearances and ask open-ended questions to confirm or rule out hypotheses.

Always share your perceptions with the project team. Understanding the position of a stakeholder becomes less subjective when you have evidence from different sources and perspectives.

The management of stakeholders' engagement begins in the planning phase; it is developed through a set of macro-activities that will be performed throughout the project until the change is institutionalized, as shown in Table 15.1.

Many of these macro-activities are meant to give meaning to the change, develop a state of psychological security, avoid the negative effects of anticipatory

Table 15.1. Stakeholder Management through Project Phases

Project phase	Macro-activity	Main goals
Planning	Define and prepare the sponsor of the project.	• Mobilize and stimulate engagement of stakeholders through clear sponsorship.
	Hold a working session to align and mobilize leaders.	• Ensure that the company leadership is aligned and champion of the change. • Mobilize co-sponsors, raising the leaders' awareness of their role as active agents of change. • Observe behaviors and evaluate potential antagonists among company leadership.
	Define the project's purpose and identity.	• Provide the reason for the change. • Stimulate the stakeholders' emotional connection with the change.
	Map and classify the stakeholders.	• Evaluate the level of acceptance for change and define strategies to increase engagement or deal with antagonism. • Promote frequent interactions with stakeholders and asses their expectations, behaviors, and the level of engagement.
	Assess the characteristics of the organizational culture and their effects on the change.	• Provide preliminary insight into the impacts the change may create. • Identify antagonistic factors and define strategies to reduce their impacts on the change. • Identify engagement factors to be used to strengthen acceptance of the change.
	Define the roles and responsibilities of the project team.	• Avoid potential conflicts. • Align the boundaries of responsibilities, reducing speculation and uncertainty that feed antagonistic attitudes toward the project. • Increase the perception of "being part of" (belonging), involving and committing important stakeholders through the project organizational chart.
	Plan the team's membership and plan for the team's development.	• Generate psychological security. • Reduce the possibility of the project team going into the negative state of anticipatory grief.

(Continued on following page)

Table 15.1. Stakeholder Management through Project Phases (*Cont'd*)

Project phase	Macro-activity	Main goals
	Assess the predisposition to the change and its impacts.	• Identify antagonistic factors and define strategies to reduce their impact on the change • Identify engagement factors to be used to strengthen acceptance of the change.
	Establish the change management action plan.	• Promote a seamless integration between the change management plan and the project management plan. • Have a change-sustaining strategy defined and aligned among the steering committee, the PMO and project management team, and councils.
Acquisition	Define the team's additional training needs.	• Develop the knowledge of the team, stimulating psychological security and confidence in the future of the project to facilitate project team engagement.
Execution	Carry out the Project Kick-off.	• Align expectations, integrate and engage the stakeholders, share the vision of future state, objective, goals, challenges, and purpose of the project. • Provide the first step toward building project team spirit. • Drive the enthusiasm and motivation of the project team and other stakeholders. • Observe behaviors and the likely level of stakeholder acceptance of change.
	Assess organizational impacts.	• Map risks inherent to the human factor. • Identify antagonistic factors and define strategies to reduce their impact on change. • Identify engagement factors to be used to strengthen acceptance of the change. • Establish a plan to relocate the stakeholders affected by the project.
	Plan and execute learning and management of acquired knowledge.	• Develop competencies to reach operational excellence. • Stimulate stakeholders' confidence in the project deliverables. • Promote a knowledge-sharing environment.
	Confirm the stakeholders' future in the post-project phase.	• Stimulate psychological security. • Reduce the possibility of the project team going into the negative state of anticipatory grief.
	Define roles and responsibilities for the production phase.	• Avoid potential conflicts. • Align the boundaries of responsibilities, reducing speculation and uncertainty that feed antagonistic attitudes toward the change during the production phase.

(Continued on following page)

Table 15.1. Stakeholder Management through Project Phases (*Cont'd*)

Project phase	Macro-activity	Main goals
Implementation	Assess stakeholders' readiness and confidence to implement the project.	• Assess logical aspects of readiness for change, such as indicators, goals, and metrics to be presented at the implementation decision meeting. • Evaluate the team's level of confidence and develop actions to enhance it when necessary.
	Ensure all leaders' commitment to the implementation.	• Anticipate possible issues that might jeopardize the implementation, address the logical ones or prepare contingencies. • Identify potential antagonistic stakeholders and their opinions and prepare actions to deal with them.
Closing	Recognize team and individual performances.	• Institutionalize the culture of continuing organizational transformation.
	Ensure adequate reassignment of project members.	• Reinforce the perception that projects are opportunities for career development, thus ensuring engagement in future changes.
	Celebrate wins and goals achieved.	• Institutionalize the culture of continuing organizational transformation. • Keep up enthusiasm to sustain the change during the production phase.

grief, and involve and mobilize people, creating a positive environment for engagement of stakeholders. Other activities allow for the identification of antagonistic factors and serve to monitor the likely level of stakeholders' acceptance of the proposed change.

Stakeholders should be monitored throughout the project and even after the end of it, as their positioning can vary greatly during the execution phase and even after the change has been implemented. Remember that when we talk about stakeholders, we are including not only those who participate in the project directly, but all those who are affected by the change, including those outside the organization.

Pay special attention to those who would like to participate but for some reason are not part of the project team. Their tendency is to vent their frustration in the form of antagonistic behaviors. Strive to keep these stakeholders engaged through direct and active communication, and if possible, explain to them why they were not on the team in a way that you conveys that you still value their ideas and inputs.

A good monitoring practice is to conduct briefing and debriefing sessions for meetings and events involving important stakeholders. During the briefing, clearly define the strategy for conducting the meeting, as well as highlighting the interactions and questions that may be raised. Be ready for the negative interventions of antagonists and define tactics to deal with them. Assign project team members as observers to monitor the behavior of meeting participants, paying attention to every detail, such as body posture, level of attention and concentration, participation, enthusiasm, etc.

During the debriefing session, discuss with the project management team the perceptions collected. Use the Stakeholder Map as a guide to document their positioning and develop strategies to expand engagement or deal with antagonists.

Monitoring stakeholders' behavior is always a challenge when you have to deal with virtual teams. The best option is to train someone on the virtual team to perform this task. Usually there is at least one person from Human Resources working closely with the virtual team. If this is your situation, negotiate the participation of this person as a part-time member of the change management team.

The recurrent macro-activities are also excellent sources of information about the level of acceptance of the change. Observe the following points in relation to these activities.

Plan and Manage Communication

Communication is an essential element to help in understanding the vision of the organization after the change, the purpose (why we are changing), what will change and how it will be changed. Communicating properly reduces organizational noise and uncertainties, adjusts expectations, and aligns stakeholders throughout the project.

In its recurring aspect, communication keeps people connected with the change and generates the perspective of transparency, reducing fear of the unknown.

Remember that much of the communication will not be planned. The change manager should address directly those who show some level of resistance in order to seek feedback and check whether:

- ❑ Messages have been properly understood.
- ❑ Situations have created discomfort.
- ❑ Needs have not been addressed.
- ❑ Situations encouraged psychological insecurity.
- ❑ Negative perceptions toward the adjustments required for expanding engagement are harbored.

A good practice in individual and face-to-face communication is to ask for recommendations. People feel flattered and valued when someone asks their help.

Apply Participatory Processes

For most people, participatory processes have a great impact on their sense of belonging. What is produced in a participatory manner generates a perception of "parenthood," including the DNA of each participant in the decisions. If they have your DNA, they are your children. If they are your children, they are beautiful by definition. You will never see someone post a picture of his or her child on social media that says, "Look how ugly my baby is!"

Encourage the use of participatory processes to generate the connection of stakeholders with the change, but be sure to observe good practices for this activity.

Manage Conflicts

Frequent logical conflicts, which are solved with a collaborative approach, may indicate that the parties are engaged. These conflicts are actually the result of an effort to find the best solutions for the change to be successful.

However, frequent psychological conflicts involving the same stakeholder may indicate discomfort and resistance to the change.

Manage Motivation

The high motivation of a team toward a project indicates engagement. However, even a motivated team can have a less motivated member. In this case, try to understand the root cause; it may be related to various personal factors that are not necessarily linked to the project.

On the other hand, low motivation, which can be the result of several factors, must be assessed against the discomfort caused by the change. If it is related to the project, first see if you can find out the root cause; otherwise, see if you can reassign this person to another position in the organization that he or she would enjoy. Remember: One negative team member can destroy the morale of the rest of the team, so in such a situation, act quickly to resolve the situation.

Manage Behaviors

Similar to motivation, inappropriate or inadequate behaviors can result from various causes.

A few years ago, we were working on a high-impact change project when we noticed that a particular person had begun to show aggressive behavior toward some stakeholders who were directly involved in the project. We began to investigate the root cause of this behavior. We found out that this person was going through a divorce and fighting with his wife for custody of their children. That situation alone would be reason enough to understand his behavioral change. To make matters worse, his wife also worked at the company and was part of the project. The targets of his aggressiveness were the stakeholders closest to his wife, who were supporting her in a personal matter, which ended up extending into the context of project interactions.

Only a deep approach to the root cause of the problem can help to understand whether the inappropriate behavior of a stakeholder is indeed related to the discomfort resulting from change. However, this is not an easy task. To be effective, you have to develop a trust relationship with the stakeholders and cultivate a high-credibility profile. If you do not feel comfortable approaching a person directly, try to figure out what could be the root cause through frank conversation with someone close to this person. When necessary demand support from HR department members. They may have some undisclosed information about the person in question and can support you in such cases.

Techniques to Reduce Antagonistic Actions

Stakeholder engagement strategies cannot be based solely on rational principles. Although the communication may be adequate and people understand that the change is necessary, you may still not achieve a high level of engagement among all stakeholders. Even if you develop all the traditional training activities and use incentive and recognition mechanisms, a small part of the stakeholder group may still feel uncomfortable with the change. We are human beings, and, as such, we are deeply complex and influenced not only by reason but also by emotion.

Do not underestimate the power of personal agendas. Each person has his or her own professional life plan, which is connected with his or her personal ambitions. Personal agendas have a tremendous impact, especially on the changes that touch the undeclared interests of some stakeholders.

There are cases where antagonism is not connected with the change. Anyone who stands out in managing a large project will face resistors whose sole intention is not to support the success of someone who competes with him or her for space in the company. The hierarchical pyramid of organizations naturally encourages competition for the few high-ranking positions.

Ego clashes, fights for power and status, are part of complex human behavior and directly influence stakeholders' support or antagonistic position.

Although focused on engagement strategies, this complexity is why stakeholder engagement needs to consider other approaches at least to reduce the action of antagonists. These approaches include induced protagonism, persuasive tactics, and extreme measures.

Induced Protagonism

Induced protagonism refers to removing antagonists from the conflict zone and placing them in the solution zone. Since engaging 100% of people is rarely possible, managing resistance and placing stakeholders in a weak position to resist the change is a viable approach that often brings great results.

When an antagonist is one of the important project stakeholders, give visibility to his or her work, make him or her take part in a council, let him or her present the progress of the activities under his or her responsibility, and create exposure to the highest hierarchical levels of the organization. When placed in such a situation, a leader who should be an agent of change but acts as an antagonist will have little strength to resist the project, even if he or she does not adhere to it.

A common mistake of project management teams is to take upon themselves the task of presenting status reports to the steering committee. Take the facilitator or moderator role. Set up the agenda and open the meeting, but make the leaders of each area be the protagonists and present their part. No one wants to appear as a resistor of the change before a steering committee. Imagine leaders who do not send their teams to the scheduled training. If it is clear that they will present the indicators for their area to a steering committee in person, chances are that these leaders will change their tactics so as not to damage their images. If the Risk Map indicates a situation that can have an effect on the change, do not allow an antagonist to put himself or herself in the position of victim. Rather, coordinate with the sponsor the need for all business areas to present their contingency plans.

In addition, there are people who feel that the change will affect their status in the organization and who would like to be in the project but are not. If they are important stakeholders, find them a space, as a member of a council, for example. The perception of exclusion deeply affects the self-esteem of people. Including them may change their perception of the change.

Remove antagonists from the problem area and include them in the solution area. You will not engage them immediately, but the survival instinct will limit their capacity to resist the change if they are induced to act as a protagonist.

Persuasive Tactics

Imposed changes leave deep marks on the organizational culture and rarely lead the company to achieve the level of excellence expected with a change. However, there are cases where the level of resistance of a stakeholder may require a persuasive approach. For example, a low-pressure approach can be used, requiring support from a proponent stakeholder who was identified as an influencer of a particular antagonist. Ask the influencer to listen to your concerns and talk about the positive dimensions of the change with the antagonist.

Medium-pressure approaches may include the involvement of Human Resources or a mentor to strengthen the company's expectation that its leaders must act as mobilizing agents of change. Reinforce the importance of the leaders acting consistently with the vision of the organization's future state; remember that what inspires a workforce is the example, not the words.

As to high-pressure approaches, they should have the support of the project sponsor and/or steering committee in an open and direct manner. At this point, persuasion will touch the border of coercion, but, if this is necessary for the success of the change, be sure to do it.

Extreme Measures

Keeping an important stakeholder for the project who does not engage and remains resistant even after using all possible tactics to isolate his or her antagonism is a lose–lose game. This scenario is poor for the stakeholder, for the result of the change, and for the organization.

This person will be in a state of misery that is likely to affect his or her productivity and career opportunities in the organization.

The change is likely to be affected and the organization sets a dangerous precedent. Its culture will carry the mark of condescension, and future changes will be much more difficult.

Extreme cases require extreme measures. Discuss with the project team the effects of this stakeholder's positioning on the success of the project. Organize evidence of his or her extreme resistance to the change, list all actions taken to isolate the opposition, and discuss the possibility of removing this person from the project or even from the organization.

Situations of this type have generally produced so much wear and tear and have involved so many people from the organization's top management that the project team's proposition will not seem an unfounded extreme measure.

Avoid extreme measures as much as possible, but do not miss the main focus, which is the institutionalization of the change. Not all will adapt to the organization's future vision. In the end, it is neither the strongest nor the most intelligent who survive, but the ones who adapt better.

Activities

- ➤ Ensure that the sponsor will widely communicate the vision of the organization's future state.
- ➤ Involve the organization's leaders to get explicit and unconditional co-sponsorship.
- ➤ Assess the expectations of key stakeholders in individual or small group meetings. In the project execution phase, evaluate how much these expectations will be met and provide feedback to ensure the key stakeholders' expectations alignment with the project outcome.
- ➤ Monitor, dynamically update, and define strategies to encourage engagement or restrict antagonistic actions using the Stakeholder Map.
- ➤ Continuously monitor the behavior of the most influential stakeholders.
- ➤ Discuss perceptions of the level of engagement of stakeholders with the project team in order to obtain different perspectives.
- ➤ Manage communications, paying attention to the need for extraordinary (unplanned), formal, and informal communications
- ➤ Develop trust and transparency with stakeholders and approach them, when necessary, to help in understanding the root cause of resistance.
- ➤ Conduct briefing and debriefing sessions in meetings with stakeholders who are important for the project.
- ➤ Use the recurring macro-activities as sources of information on the behavior of stakeholders and their level of acceptance of the change.
- ➤ Apply techniques to reduce antagonistic actions:
  - ○ Induced protagonism
  - ○ Persuasive tactics
  - ○ Extreme measures

Chapter 16

CMO—The Change Management Office

16.1. Turning Strategy into Results

Many companies invest valuable top management time developing strategic plans, but few succeed in executing them properly. According to Chris Zook and James Allen (2010), seven out of eight companies in a global sample of nearly 2,000 large organizations have not been successful in increasing their profitability as planned in strategic initiatives.

In the view of Robert S. Kaplan and David P. Norton (2005), creators of the Balanced Scorecard (BSC), the problem is related to the gap between the formulation and implementation of the strategy. Their research shows that, on average, 95% of employees of an organization are unaware of the strategy, which makes its implementation much more difficult. Moreover, in 67% of the organizations, HR and IT managers develop activities without aligning them with the strategic plan. The bonuses of employees in more than 90% of cases have no connection with the success or failure of the strategic initiatives.

Kaplan and Norton suggest that creating an Office of Strategy Management (OSM) is a good practice to increase the effective implementation of strategy. This new organizational function is not the same one that coordinates the development of the strategic plan, but rather it is a complement focused on managing the implementation of the strategy, which will involve processes, technology, and people. This approach implies aligning various departments, such as Human

Resources (HR), Information Technology (IT), Project Management Office (PMO), Process Improvement (PI) or Quality Control (QC), and Finance. The last must ensure that the budget of each department and business unit will also be aligned with the corporate strategy.

When we talk about strategy implementation, we are talking about change. It is within this strategic context that we recommend an organizational function, the Change Management Office (CMO).

16.2. The Concept of the CMO

The CMO is an organizational function that has gained strength as the practice of managing the human factor in change processes is recognized as a discipline essential to the success of organizations.

The CMO can be defined as an area of the company that supports developing the strategy, prioritizing the project portfolio, managing the methodology, best practices, and tools, as well as planning, conducting, monitoring, and supporting organizational change through its interactions with other functions connected to the planning and execution of the organization's strategy.

Implementing a CMO almost always results from the maturation of the organizational change management discipline in a company. In general, change management techniques begin to be used by a department—usually IT or HR—and later, when they have generated perceived value because of the project's results, they evolve into a broader role, establishing the CMO as a specialized area that covers all the changes within an organization.

Similar to the Project Management Office (PMO), the CMO has different levels of maturity and importance in different organizations. In most organizations, change management is still at a primary level of operational performance during the project execution phase, and it is focused exclusively on communication and training. In organizations that begin structuring a CMO, it may operate as a small unit formed by few people, usually as a part of the PMO In organizations that have achieved a certain level of excellence in their governance model, the CMO is formed by structures that are connected directly to the highest hierarchical levels responsible for defining and implementing corporate strategy. In these cases we often find an area dedicated to the coordination of the dynamic planning of the strategy and the management of its execution. The CMO is explicitly sponsored by the CEO and other members of the C-suite, working from the strategic plan, integrated with other areas of the organization, such as HR, IT, PMO, PI or QC, and Finance.

Table 16.1 shows how the CMO evolves as the level of change management matures within an organization.

Table 16.1. Change Management Maturity Levels and the CMO

Level of Maturity	Characteristics	Change Management Focus
1. Primary	Typical of organizations where the PMO does not exist, and project management is focused only on time, cost, and scope.	When change management is applied, its focus is limited to communication and training in a specific project, without integration with the project management methodology.
2. Operational	Usually exists in organizations that have departmental PMOs acting more as controllers of project implementation.	Change management is applied in some projects. Although this role is operational, there is an awareness of the need to assess organizational impacts and basic stakeholder engagement techniques.
3. Pattern-oriented	Found in organizations that, even having departmental PMOs, apply a standardized methodology. The role of the PMO is also advisory.	Change management follows a pattern and is integrated with project management. Some leadership levels understand the importance of managing the human factor in order to have successful projects.
4. Tactical management	Organizations at this level of maturity generally have a structured PMO with a corporate role that includes the change management concepts in its methodology.	CMO exists as part of the PMO structure. All projects have explicit sponsorship of leaders. Change management operates in projects at the strategic level from the planning phase.
5. Strategic performance	The PMO is a function integrated with the strategy-execution area. Its function is to ensure the execution of the project and program methodologies and the portfolio of projects, aiming at achieving strategic objectives. The PMO and CMO act in an integrated manner to take the organization to its vision of the future state.	The CMO appears as an organizational function at the same level as the PMO, both integrated with strategy execution and other functions such as HR, IT, PMO, PI or QC, and Finance. Its mission also involves predicting the need for change projects to enable the vision of the organization's future state. The project portfolio is prioritized and developed, taking into account organizational impacts assessed in the strategic planning. The CMO has an advisory role in the projects underway in the organization.

16.3. The Role of the CMO

The role of the CMO depends on the level of maturity of change management in the organization. As we have seen, organizational change management can vary from a simple operating unit to an entire area (the CMO) with a tactical and strategic role.

Organizations with a high level of maturity in their governance model think not only about the strategy but also about the plan to execute it. The human factor and the organizational culture are factors that are also taken into account as part of the modeling that will lead the organization to a higher competitive level in the short term, and in its continuous organizational transformation process.

The sequence and speed with which changes will be implemented are factors considered when the strategy is turned into one of portfolio management, so that the excessive level of discomfort that these changes may cause does not overload people.

If, on one hand, we live in a world that demands more and more change, and on the other hand, we have a workforce that is unable to absorb and actually assimilate the change, it then threatens the execution of the strategic demands from portfolio management.

Organizations that can implement a large number of changes in a short period of time are those that, at some earlier stage of their strategic approach, prioritized forming a "resilient organization," that is, an organization with an organizational culture in which its leaders and people in the organization are prepared to live with continual change.

These organizations respond faster to market demands, without taking their workforce to a level of psychological insecurity that increases resistance to any one proposed change. This ability to change paradigms is not the result of chance, but of a culture that strategically planned to reach this level of organizational maturity.

The role of the CMO in the strategic planning process and in the portfolio management process derivation of a project portfolio needs to be coordinated with other organizational functions such as HR, IT, PMO, PI or QC, and the strategic plan execution team. Figure 16.1 presents these relationships as part of an integrated strategic planning pyramid.

The strategic role of the CMO identifies and articulates the gap between the current and future states from the human point of view. Preliminary impacts can be anticipated, enabling the organization to estimate the effort in terms of change management and the prioritized strategic initiatives.

For example, in an organization with an expansion strategy based on acquisitions, the CMO should assess the impact of this decision on the organization and its workforce, and then identify and coordinate projects to prepare the

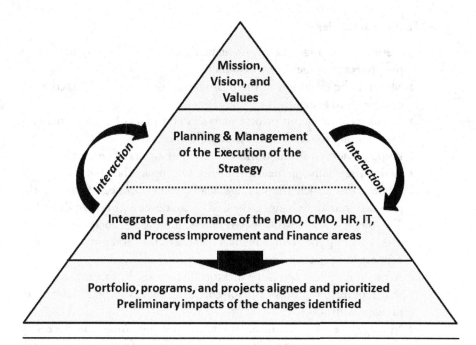

Figure 16.1   Integrated strategic planning.

leaders and the workforce to deal with the cultural merger that will occur after an acquisition. Similarly, the PI, HR, and IT functions will have to revisit other CMO-identified initiatives to prepare the organization for the success of this new strategy. The budget process coordinated by the finance area should be in line with all of these strategic initiatives.

The portfolio of programs and projects needs to be aligned with the sentence that defines the organization's vision, that is, how the organization wants to be within a given timeframe. To achieve its vision, the organization will require several changes, some with high impact and others with small impact. Some elements of the culture will demand adjustments, and others will have to be replaced or inserted so that the vision is achieved and sustained.

A CMO that performs the tactical management of change has already taken a major step forward for an organization. Although it focuses on the execution of the projects, it also addresses human issues in organizational change and adds value to ensure that the strategic objectives that motivated the venture are achieved.

The following list outlines the tactical and strategic activities to be undertaken by the CMO.

➢ **Tactical activities**

- ❑ Define the change management methodology and integrate it with the project management methodology.
- ❑ Monitor the evolution of the techniques, tools, and best practices of change management.
- ❑ Act as a disseminator of best practices and tools of change management among the leaders of the organization.
- ❑ Prepare leaders and the workforce to act as agents of change.
- ❑ Assign the change management team to support the projects.
- ❑ Review and enrich the Change Management Strategic Plan for the projects; in major changes, the CMO can develop this plan directly.
- ❑ Together with the PMO, be part of the monitoring process of the projects, assessing the change management activities and providing direct support to projects where necessary.
- ❑ Act as the project sponsor's mentor, discussing the critical situations that require the sponsor's involvement to increase engagement or to manage conflicts.
- ❑ Manage the change sustainability phase, providing the necessary resources to ensure the adjustments required after the project goes into production. Report project achievements and the change consolidation level to the strategic planning area.

➢ **Strategic activities**

- ❑ Assess the vision of the future state planned for the organization and its strategic plan, and suggest projects needed to prepare for the planned changes.
- ❑ Participate in discussions promoted by the function responsible for planning and executing the strategy, evaluating from the very first moment the organizational impact of the strategic initiatives.
- ❑ Participate in prioritization of the organization's portfolio as a member of the Portfolio Review Board or similar oversight group.
- ❑ Interact with HR to evaluate the opportunities provided by each project to strengthen, or incorporate values into, the organizational culture.
- ❑ Assess the preliminary impacts of the change to the portfolio, defining priorities and estimating the number of change personnel needed as well as other investments.
- ❑ Interact with the other areas involved in the execution of the strategy, such as HR, IT, PMO, PI or QC, and Finance, to ensure alignment of all initiatives with the organization's strategic plan.

16.4. Where to Establish the CMO

Where should the CMO be established? Some change management experts argue that the CMO must be connected to the top management of the organization, because it is critical for the development of the strategy. Others believe that the CMO should be part of Human Resources, because HR is linked directly both to engagement in the change process and to the effects a change project can have on the organizational culture. There are also those who assert that the CMO should be established in the project, PI, or IT area. We believe that the most natural way is the evolution of a single cell of change management working in a project to a CMO initially established in a department. As the CMO becomes more mature and shows its value, it evolves to a position linked to strategy execution in the organizational structure.

Regardless of where the CMO is established, it is important that the CMO understands its advisory role. It is not an auditor or interventionist. Its focus should be on working in harmony with the various functions that interact with the execution of strategic plans, so that the portfolio can take the organization to its planned future vision.

A few years ago I worked with a major global organization that had established a CMO directed by a member from the top of the hierarchical structure. This global organization was growing at an incredible rate through acquisitions and new business development, having doubled its revenues in a little more than eight years. Interestingly, the CMO was seen by the PMO not as a partner to face the challenges of the numerous projects underway, but as a "foreign body"—an interventionist that hindered more than it helped. One clash between the project and change managers of a large-scale project that would affect much of the organization in different geographic locations led to a strange and disruptive situation. While one player asserted that the Project Kick-off should be centralized (as was the project), the other would not give up the notion of a regional Project Kick-off for each major center where the organization operated. Incredible as it may seem, after much discussion the time for the project to be launched arrived; the organization ended up having two kick-offs: one organized by the project management team and another by the change management team.

This is a good example of how lack of integration between different functions that work on change projects can be a risk factor and not a value-added factor.

After experiencing projects with organizations of different sizes having different cultures, we believe that two factors influence the creation and evolution of the CMO in an organization:

1. The positioning of HR
2. The level of maturity of the PMO and strategy management

1. **The positioning of HR**
   Organizations where HR still has a purely tactical and operational role tend to have more difficulty in sensitizing top management about the need for orchestrated change. In many cases, HR does not even realize the importance of organizational change management, which greatly complicates establishing a CMO. In these organizations, the culture is usually not planned and developed through HR initiatives. The organizational culture has just evolved organically from a set of beliefs, practiced values, myths, style of leadership, and people management models—aspects that have not been articulated or consciously implemented.

   When HR plays a strategic role in the organization, it not only encourages the development of the change management practice, it may also establish the CMO as part of its organizational structure. In cases where the CMO is linked directly to the strategic planning area, HR interacts with both the CMO and the PMO to include programs and projects in the portfolio, based on the strategy, or to take advantage of the opportunities brought by other initiatives to orchestrate the evolution of the organizational culture.

2. **The level of maturity of the PMO and strategy management**
   Organizations that still treat the PMO as an operational function that controls project execution rarely have a CMO. When they do, the PMO is actually a function or a small department within an area of the business, or the PMO acts alone in one project or another without using those projects to develop the organizational culture.

   By contrast, those organizations having a firm understanding that strategy is executed by turning strategic initiatives into a portfolio of programs and projects, with implementation managed by a corporate PMO, realize more quickly the importance of having a CMO as a catalyst for efforts related to the human factor in the changes demanded by the strategy itself. Generally, each initiative is also used to strengthen or implement aspects of the desired organizational culture. The success rate of the projects, in relation to the fulfillment of their strategic objectives is greater, therefore making the organization more competitive, profitable, and long-lived.

The best position the CMO can have in the organizational structure is one that values and maintains integration with Human Resources, Information Technology, the Project Management Office, Process Improvement or Quality Control, and Finance, working directly in the execution of the organization's strategy.

16.5. Examples of CMO Structures

Here are two models that we believe are appropriate for the CMO's position in the organizational structure and its main features. Remember that these are just two examples of structure. Many others may be applied. The best model will be the one that fits into an organization's culture, generating integration and cooperation between the functions responsible for implementing the project portfolio, thus ensuring execution of the corporate strategy.

Model A

In Figure 16.2, the CMO occupies a position linked directly to the function that coordinates the planning and managing of strategy execution. The change management team operates as part of the project team, reporting to the project manager and, according to the organizational matrix, to the CMO. The HR, PI, and Finance functions may or may not have representatives in this same structure. If they have, there will be more synergy. If they do not, it is necessary to create integration protocols for any organizational transformation to happen in a structured way, in harmony with all these positions in the organizational structure. Figure 16.2 represents the most evolved model of this approach. The PMO and CMO are part of the function that articulates the planning and managing of strategy execution, where HR, IT, PI, and Finance also have representatives.

Model B

In Figure 16.3, the PMO and CMO are farther away from the portfolio function that coordinates the strategy planning and execution. The CMO is positioned within the HR function, while the PMO is part of the IT function (the PMO could be in the PI function or any other). This model has a greater potential for the PMO and CMO to have a more tactical than a strategic approach. In this figure we can see that even having the CMO and PMO in different functions assumes that the change management team reports to the project manager and, according to the organizational matrix, to the CMO. A common effect of segregating the CMO from the PMO is a subversion of this model, placing change managers and project managers at the same hierarchical level. This sets the scene for potential conflicts and disputes between the PMO and the CMO, which often hinders more than helps achievement of the strategic objectives of a project. In this model, the interaction with the finance function is almost always restricted to the function responsible for the strategy, and there is no interaction with the CMO, PMO, HR, IT, and PI in the execution of the portfolio.

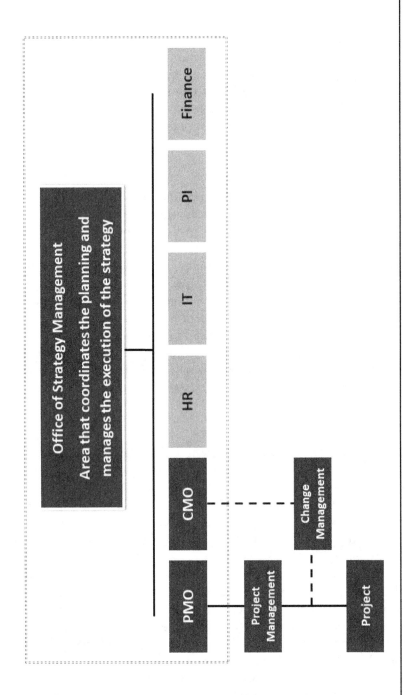

Figure 16.2 Model A—Positioning of CMO and PMO.

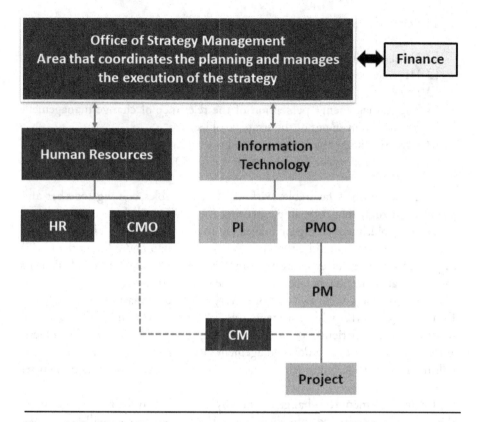

Figure 16.3   Model B—Alternative positioning of CMO and PMO.

16.6. Implementing a CMO is a Project and Requires Change Management

The implementation of a CMO is a project that introduces a new element in the organizational structure. It must be developed as a change project, considering the impacts on human factor issues such as power, status, and discomfort with the new. If the change management discipline is not yet part of the organization's culture, the challenge will be even greater, as the project management approach will also be impacted.

Plan the CMO implementation as a project that will go through all of the usual phases, from planning to execution and into production—an effort that will certainly require support for the change to be institutionalized.

This project, as any other, features unique characteristics. The Change Management Strategic Plan activities must take into account factors such as:

❏ Level of maturity of the change management discipline in the organization and its history of performance in projects
❏ Level of maturity of the PMO
❏ HR role model—strategic or tactical/operational
❏ Level of maturity of the strategy planning and execution process
❏ Top management's perception of the relevance of change management for the achievement of the strategic objectives
❏ Organizational change history and organizational culture
❏ C-suite support for implementing the CMO

If the situation is favorable, with all these variables coming together and resulting in high maturity, implementing the CMO will be a natural move, seen as an evolution of change management in the organization. However, if the situation is not as favorable, the need exists to develop and address the CMO as part of a process of evolving the organization's governance model. Plan its implementation in phases together with the other entities involved.

You cannot skip steps and go from a very low level of maturity to excellence. Establishing a CMO with a strategic role is part of a structured plan that will require time and patience, persuasiveness, engagement of various stakeholders, and sponsorship from senior management. Remember, this is a high-impact cultural change that will touch on sensitive paradigms and issues such as power and status.

If you implement the change too rapidly, advancing to the next phase before the former is assimilated into the organizational culture, you will be exposed as someone who is creating an uncomfortable situation for other stakeholders you need for support. Remember, "The horse is fast and slender, but the camel marches night and day."

The following list contains activities that will help to plan the evolution of change management until a CMO with a strategic role is achieved:

➢ Integrate the change management approach into the project management methodology.
➢ Develop trust with the change management team and PMO; act in an integrated manner. Make them see you as a partner who is part of the project management team and not as a competitor.
➢ Define the boundaries of performance of the change management function with HR to avoid conflicts.
➢ Disseminate change management practices by training project managers, process professionals, HR, and IT.
➢ Establish the vision of the future of change management in the organization and plan its continued evolution.

> ➤ Find a sponsor with high influence in the organization.
> ➤ Define indicators to monitor the evolution of change management in the organization and communicate them.
> ➤ Develop the performance of change management from lower maturity levels to maturity level 3—pattern-oriented. Even for this development, you need sponsorship from areas such as HR, IT, and/or the PMO. If possible, seek support from the area of portfolio management.
> ➤ Sensitize leaders to the need for evolution of the governance model to include the planning and implementation of the organization's strategy to be more effective in achieving its strategic objectives.
> ➤ Coordinate the joint evolution of the areas that, in a new governance model, will act in an integrated manner to support the planning and implementation of the strategy—PMO, CMO, HR, IT, PI, and Finance.
> ➤ Use benchmarks from independent sources to show the relevance of the CMO for the business. Avoid using studies from specialized consultants. They can be interpreted as biased, even when they are not. This will affect the credibility of your sale for a strategic CMO, and reversing this situation will not be easy.

Chapter 17

Essential Competencies for Change Leaders

Leadership is the activity of influencing people to strive willingly for group objectives.

– George R. Terry (1977)

The era of information, knowledge, speed, and "disposables" has exposed people to constant change. This context requires developing skills such as flexibility and resilience, previously not considered essential, to be able to adapt continuously to the new status quo. These skills are relevant to everyone, but they are particularly essential for leaders.

However, because of human nature and its complexity, psychological, cognitive, and emotional processes, each individual needs a different time span for maturing. The change leader needs to understand and develop strategies to deal with the different periods of time each individual involved in the change will take to engage.

A group of individuals does not presuppose a team, especially a working team. It is the responsibility of any leader to form teams that work in unison. The challenge to the change leader goes further: He or she needs to maintain team cohesion in a time of transformation and often uncertainty.

The change leader is a professional with skills to align, inspire, enliven, motivate, get commitment, and guide people. He or she gives direction, helps create a purpose, checks the way, and informs the destination and the meaning of the tasks and actions, balancing individual and collective projects. He or she is a catalyst capable of accelerating the organizational change process and promoting individual and team engagement toward the new purposes.

17.1. A Definition of Competency

When we think of competencies, we should consider the KAA model (Rabaglio, 2008), where K, for Knowledge, refers to the technical learning acquired through life, in schools, universities, courses, and other sources of learning (the cognitive domain); A, for ability, refers to the know-how-to-do, which is the capacity to carry out a certain task, physical or intellectual (the psychomotor domain); and A, for Attitude, refers to the want-to-do, which refers to our behaviors in situations and tasks of our day-to-day life (the affective domain). It is closely connected to intrinsic motivation and emotional intelligence.

We allow ourselves to expand the KAA model to KAASE, where S, for Sense, has to do with knowing the why-to-do, the capacity to think about something and identify the sense of purpose (the creative/reflexive domain); and E, for Energy, is the capacity to inspire and promote infectious enthusiasm in the team.

We live today in a state of impermanence. In this context, it is necessary that managers and leaders perform similarly to conductors preparing for and giving a concert—communicating the song to be played, the audience profile, and the role of each instrument, directing the performance so that all individuals together provide an excellent concert. This is the true and indispensable change leader that all modern-day companies need.

17.2. Competencies for Change Leaders

Given our KAASE model, we have defined eight competencies for change leaders that do not include, but assume, any technical knowledge required for the business. Table 17.1 lists these competencies, which are explained in the following paragraphs.

Table 17.1. Essential Competencies for Change Leaders

Sensitivity to human factors and astuteness to unveil them; empathic attitude
Capacity to facilitate, inspire, and encourage team effort
A focus on results, goals, and productivity
Ability to plan and negotiate—strategic vision
Ability to manage conflicts, crises, and opportunities
Creativity, inquisitiveness, boldness, and willingness to break paradigms
Effectiveness as a communicator; a good listener
Transparency, credibility, and integrity

17.2.1. Sensitivity to Human Factors and Astuteness to Unveil Them; Empathic Attitude

Of all the skills required for a change manager, this is the most important. We called the Body of Knowledge presented here, "Human Change Management," because it is human beings with all their complexity who are the main characters involved in change. Human reactions, moods, motivations, behaviors, and engagement will determine their interaction with the change—whether it will be positive or not. An effective change manager is many things. Some critical characteristics include:

- ❏ An insightful person with the sensitivity to understand what is not clearly expressed, what is hidden in the more apparent side of an attitude
- ❏ A shrewd enough observer to read in everyone's eyes their frame of mind in relation to the moment of the project
- ❏ Someone who understands the factors that influence behaviors and finds solutions to situations that, in general, are more psychological than logical
- ❏ Someone who can put himself or herself in another's shoes to understand the feelings and emotions from the perspective of others. Having an empathic attitude is an essential element for the high-performance change manager.

17.2.2. Capacity to Facilitate, Inspire, and Encourage Team Effort

The change manager must be an inspiring leader, capable of conveying the purpose of the change and leading people toward their motivation to engage; a person capable of turning pessimistic visions and apparently negative settings into positive ones—a facilitator to reconcile the interests of the different stakeholders. Sometimes a change leader is a pacifier, capable of thinking about the multiple aspects of an issue—whether it is a vendor or a customer issue as an example—and working with the project management team so that the human issues are not excluded from the purpose of the project but are reconciled with it.

17.2.3. A Focus on Results, Goals, and Productivity

A project is born from an objective and, even if it deals with the human factor, the change manager's main commitment is to the project's results, goals, and productivity. Change management is the discipline that maximizes project results through human factors while influencing a cultural evolution for an organization that grows and develops through continuous learning. These are the reasons why the change manager exists. The change manager is not a good friend who participates in a change to defend or protect people. The focus on results will often require the change manager to make difficult decisions such as replacing or even suggesting the dismissal of fierce antagonists who, even with all the techniques applied, insist on resisting the purpose of the project, hindering the development of the organization.

17.2.4. Ability to Plan and Negotiate—Strategic Vision

Planning is the most delicate phase of a change. The effects of the planning phase will be felt throughout the project, hence the importance of strategic thinking and the ability to plan. A well-carried-out planning phase can tremendously increase team engagement and reduce resistance, creating a clear, logical, and transparent purpose for the stakeholders. Even so, the dynamics of a change project will require several negotiations as unforeseen factors inevitably arise. Even elements such as deadlines and project team assignments will require the ability to negotiate with stakeholders, including the project sponsor. The change manager's ability to develop positions capable of persuading the parties involved will be the basis for a fair negotiation that leads to gains, reconciling the various interests at stake. Strategic vision is the ability that allows the change manager to understand the different settings and, before helping to establish a purpose, understand the greater strategy behind the objective to be pursued. This strategic view of a project will influence several activities, including communications management, facilitation, conflict management, inspiration and encouragement, and maintaining focus on results.

17.2.5. Ability to Manage Conflicts, Crises, and Opportunities

Conflicts and crises are inherent in any change process. The ability to act in advance and turn them into opportunities is a competency that influences the environment of the project, considerably increasing the chances of success. The change manager must be clever to deal with these adversities, being able to understand the different perspectives that lead to conflict or crisis in order to manage them. The change manager must be able to isolate logical from psychological conflicts and create strategies to resolve them. Behind crises and conflicts there is always a learning opportunity or improvement, be it in a process, business rule, or even human behavior.

17.2.6. Creativity, Inquisitiveness, Boldness, and Willingness to Break Paradigms

Creativity is a competency that supports the change manager's overall performance. It allows the change manager to find alternatives during times when issues seem unsolvable. A creative person is naturally inquisitive. This is the only way he or she can think differently and seek the unusual. His or her prevailing thinking before paradigms is not "Why?" but "Why not?" His or her evident mark is low attachment to the past. He or she manages the present to build the future. He or she does not try to guess the future but rather strives to create it. This is the only way he or she can understand times when old habits are keeping the organization attached to its paradigms and then can encourage the team to think differently, breaking with traditional practices.

17.2.7. Effectiveness as a Communicator; a Good Listener

The planning effort and the dynamic adaptation of communication are essential qualities to promote team engagement. Having an excellent purpose is not enough; it is necessary to communicate it effectively. Maintaining team cohesion has a lot to do with keeping the team well informed and managing expectations in a transparent and objective way. It is necessary to have a clear view of what to communicate and how. One must define the situations for using direct mass or individual communication in order to be persuasive. As communication presupposes a two-way street, the change manager needs to be a good listener, as well as being perceived as a good listener. He or she must intelligently create the channels and emotional bonds for people to feel comfortable finding him or her and expressing their emotions. His or her sensitivity to the need for the team to have a voice should allow him or her to build the formal and informal feedback channels required in all communication.

17.2.8. Transparency, Credibility, and Integrity

Transparency is connected directly to the congruence between speech and actions. There is a right time to reveal every change detail. Missing this timing eliminates the change manager's perception of transparency. On many occasions, being transparent means making it clear that a matter cannot yet be addressed. The basis for credibility lies in creating expectations that can be met. A change leader without credibility is not capable of presenting a purpose without creating mistrust, much less of generating engagement with this purpose. Credibility is built on straightforward and ethical behavior, fair and equal to everyone. Even when the change manager has to make unpopular decisions, if his or her credibility has been built on a solid basis, the team's confidence in the change manager and his or her credibility will not be affected. It is worth remembering that building a reputation of integrity to promote credibility with the team is a slow and gradual process. However, all it takes to destroy credibility is one action that is inconsistent with the message. The effect is immediate, and rebuilding credibility can take a long time.

Appendix I

The HCMBOK®
Preliminary Approach
to Agile Methodologies
in Changes Involving
Systems Development

Agile methodologies have evolved rapidly, generating new and different paradigms in project management. In general, the environment of agile methodologies values the iterative and incremental development of functionality and features, depending on priorities set by those who create the demand for the project. In short, the basic values* of the agile approach are

Individuals and interactions *over* processes and tools
Working software *over* comprehensive documentation
Customer collaboration *over* contract negotiation
Responding to change *over* following a plan

---

* Derived from the Manifesto for Agile Software Development (www.agilemanifesto.org), signed on February 17, 2001, by Kent Beck, Mike Beedle, Arie van Bennekum, Alistair Cockburn, Ward Cunningham, Martin Fowler, James Grenning, Jim Highsmith, Andrew Hunt, Ron Jeffries, Jon Kern, Brian Marick, Robert Cecil Martin, Steve Mellor, Ken Schwaber, Jeff Sutherland, and Dave Thomas.

That is, even if there is value in the items on the right, the ones on the left (in bold), are a priority. HCMBOK® has many characteristics that are congruent with agile principles and practices, including transparency, collaboration, and effective communication. Frequent face-to-face communication between the project requestor and one or more members of the project team is not only encouraged, but required, to keep the development process moving forward.

As have many entities within the software development and change management arenas, HCMBOK® has worked on the adaptation of its macro-activities to agile methodologies, one that will preserve its focus on the human factor during change while respecting the need to explore shortened project durations and still achieve critical project functionality. Figure AI.1 presents a perception of the relationship between the HCMBOK® macro-activities and the agile approach to systems development. The graphic emphasizes the iterative nature of agile development with smaller segments of functionality, while not ignoring the ongoing macro-activities as defined by HCMBOK®.

In future editions of HCMBOK®, we will have a more developed definition of the relationship between agile and our methodology.

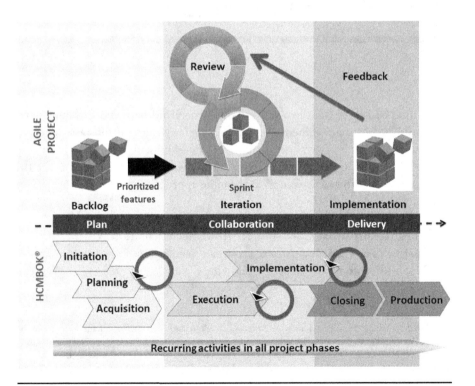

Figure AI.1   Preliminary concept of the relationship between HCMBOK® macro-activities and an agile project.

Appendix II

Organizational Culture Management and Change Management

Edgar Schein, considered an authority in organizational culture, in his book, *Organizational Culture and Leadership*, defines culture as: "A pattern of shared basic assumptions that the group learns as it solves its problems of external adaptation and internal integration that have been experienced enough to be considered valid and, therefore, worthy of being taught to new members as the correct way to perceive, think and feel about these problems" (Schein, 2010).

In this context, Schein proposes the existence of three levels of interaction among members of an organization that contribute to its culture. Figure AII.1 illustrates these three levels of interaction.

Organizations often make changes that directly involve elements of the organizational culture and carry out projects for the development of their culture. In this context, it is important to remember that cultural change requires sponsorship from the top management of the organization; it is a long-term project and should incorporate HCMBOK®'s activities to support change management. Some guidelines for planning and implementing a cultural project implementation are listed below:

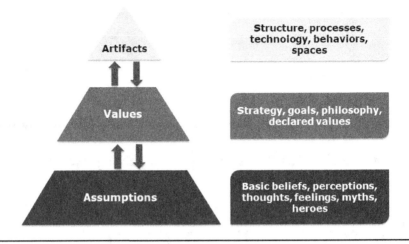

Figure AII.1   Schein's levels of cultural interaction.

> ➢ Plan the desired model of culture together with Human Resources and discuss it extensively with the leaders of the organization.
> ➢ Evaluate the culture according to one of the reference models [Denison or OCAI (Organizational Cultural Assessment Instrument), for example].
> ➢ Evaluate the dominant organizational culture but remember that there are different subcultures, which can be departmental or regional (in different geographical locations).
> ➢ Map the gap and the impacts of the change at different levels and elements of the organizational culture.
> ➢ Map the risks, opportunities, and threats related to the change of organizational culture.
> ➢ Establish and implement feedback channels to understand the evolution of the project, make adjustments, and monitor organizational learning.
> ➢ Monitor and control the project, giving emphasis to the human factors and desired organizational results through a set of indicators that show the evolution of the change.

Figure AII.2 illustrates a practical conceptual model for managing culture within an organization.

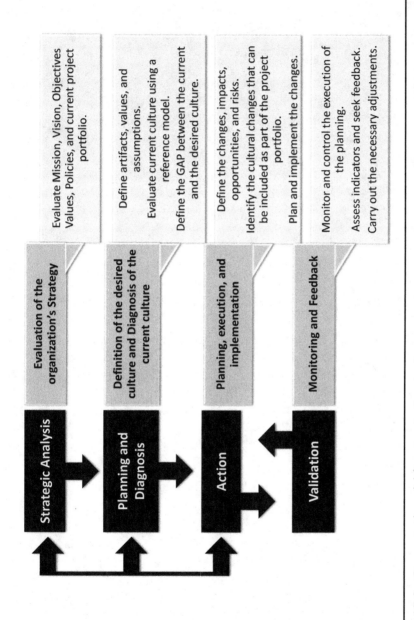

Figure AII.2 Conceptual model for organizational culture management.

Bibliography

Amabile, Teresa M. (1992). *Growing Up Creative: Nurturing a Lifetime of Creativity*. Buffalo, NY: Creative Education Foundation Press.

Bauman, Zygmunt. (2001). *Modernidade líquida*. Rio de Janeiro: Jorge Zahar.

Bohns, Vanessa K. (2017). A face-to-face request is 34 times more successful than an email. *Harvard Business Review*. https://hbr.org/2017/04/a-face-to-face-request-is-34-times-more-successful-than-an-email

Bonder, Nilton. (1995). *O segredo judaico de resolução de problemas*. Rio de Janeiro: Imago.

Bowlby, J. (1990). *Apego: A natureza do vínculo* (2ª ed.). (Álvaro Cabral, transl.). São Paulo: Martins Fontes.

Burkus, David. (2015). Why a $70,000 minimum salary isn't enough for gravity payments. *Forbes*. https://www.forbes.com/sites/davidburkus/2015/08/02/why-a-70000-minimum-salaries-isnt-enough-for-gravity-payments/#5e2c52ab5ad9

Cagé, Julia, & Angelucci, Charles. (2016). *Newspapers in Times of Low Advertising Revenues*. Centre for Economic Policy Research. http://cepr.org/active/publications/discussion_papers/dp.php?dpno=11414

Carvalho, André L., & Vilas Boas, Ana Alice. (2003). *Demissões responsáveis: O resgate das práticas originais do outplacement através da responsabilidade social*. Rio de Janeiro: I SIMGEN/UFRRJ.

Chiavenato, Idalberto. (1996). *Os novos paradigmas: Como as mudanças estão mexendo com as empresas*. São Paulo: Atlas.

Chiavenato, Idalberto. (1997). *Recursos humanos: Edição compacta*. São Paulo: Atlas.

Chiavenato, Idalberto. (1999). *Gestão de pessoas: O novo papel dos recursos humanos nas organizações*. Rio de Janeiro: Campus.

Christensen, C. (2001). *O dilema da inovação*. São Paulo: Makron Books.

Conner, Daryl R. (1992). *Managing at the Speed of Change: How Resilient Managers Succeed and Prosper Where Others Fail*. New York: Villard Books.

De Masi, Domenico. (2000). *O ócio criativo*. Rio de Janeiro: Ed. Sextante.

Delbecq, A. L., Vande De Ven, A. H., & Gustafson, D. H. (1975). *Group Techniques for Program Planning: A Guide to Nominal Group and Delphi Processes*. Glenview, IL: Scott Foresman.

Denison, Daniel, Hooijberf, Robert, Lane, Nancy, & Lief, Collen. (2012). *Leading Culture Change in Global Organizations*. San Francisco: Jossey-Bass.

Dinsmore, Paul C. (1984). *Human Factors in Project Management*. New York: Amacom.

Dornelas, José Carlos. (2001). *Empreendedorismo: Transformando ideias em negócios.* Rio de Janeiro: Elsevier.

Enriquez, Eugène. (1974). *As figuras do poder.* São Paulo: Via Lettera.

Fleury, Maria Tereza Leme, & Fischer, Rosa Maria. (1990). *Cultura e poder nas organizações.* São Paulo: Atlas.

Frankl, Viktor. (2009). *Man's Search for Meaning.* (Walter O. Schlupp & Carlos C. Avelin, transl.). São Leopoldo, Brazil: Vozes.

Gaudêncio, Paulo. (1995). *Men at Work: Como o ser humano se torna e se mantém produtivo.* São Paulo: Mennon.

Goleman, Daniel. (1995). *Inteligência emocional.* Rio de Janeiro: Objetiva.

Goleman, Daniel, Kaufman, Paul, & Ray, Michael. (1992). *Espírito criativo.* São Paulo: Cultrix Amana Key.

Hanh, Thich Nhat. (1976). *Para viver em paz, o milagre da mente alerta.* Petrópolis, Brazil: Vozes.

Hanks, Kurt. (1947, 2006). *O navegador de mudanças: Preparando um novo tipo de líder para um amanhã inexplorado.* (Eliana Chiocheti & Maria Luiza de Abreu Lima, transl.). Rio de Janeiro: Qualitymark.

Harvey, J. B. (1974). *The Abilene Paradox: The Management of Agreement.* Organizational Dynamics.

Herrmann, Ned. (1989). *The Creative Brain.* Lake Lure, NC: Brain Books.

Huet, Ellen, & Newcomer, Eric. (2016). Airbnb files to raise $850 million at $30 billion valuation. https://www.bloomberg.com/news/articles/2016-08-05/airbnb-files-to-raise-850-million-at-30-billion-valuation

Isert, Bernd. (2004). *A linguagem da mudança.* (Sabine Haraguchi, transl.). Rio de Janeiro: Qualitymark.

Jung, C. G. (1991). *Tipos psicológicos* (6th ed.). Petrópolis, Brazil: Vozes.

Kaplan, Robert, & Norton, David. (2005). *Creating the Office of Strategy Management.* Boston: Harvard Business School. http://www.hbs.edu/faculty/Publication%20Files/05-071.pdf

Land, George, & Jarman, Beth. (1998). *Breakpoint and Beyond: Mastering the Future Today.* New York: Harper Business.

Lewin, K. (1967). *Problemas de dinâmica de grupo.* São Paulo: Cultrix.

Lipp, Marilda N. (2005). *Manual do inventário de sintomas de stress para adultos de Lipp (ISSL).* São Paulo: Casapsi Livraria Editora e Gráfica.

Magalhães, Dulce. (2006). *Mensageiro do vento: Uma viagem pela mudança.* Rio de Janeiro: Qualitymark.

Marques, Sandra. (1994). Como evitar grandes traumas nos processos de mudança. In: *Recursos humanos: Excelência de ideias, prática e ação.* Rio de Janeiro: Quartet.

Maslow, Abraham H. (1968). *Introdução à psicologia do ser* (2nd ed.). Rio de Janeiro: Eldorado.

Murray, Edward J. (1983). *Motivação humana* (5th ed.). Rio de Janeiro: Zahar.

O'Brien, Henry. (2016). *Agile Project Management, A QuickStart Beginners' Guide to Mastering Agile Project Management.* Amazon—CreateSpace Independent Publishing Platform.

O'Donnell, Ken. (1994). *Raízes da transformação: A qualidade individual como base da qualidade total.* Salvador, Brazil: Casa da Qualidade.

Osborn, J. G., & Osborn, R. N. (1999). *Fundamentos de comportamento organizacional.* Porto Alegre, Brazil: Bookman.

Paulson, Terry L. (1994). *Gerentes na linha de fogo: Administrando conflitos nas relações do trabalho.* São Paulo: Saraiva.

Penna, Antônio Gomes. (1975). *Motivação e emoção.* Rio de Janeiro: Editora Rio.

PMSURVEY.ORG 2013 Edition. Project Management Institute.

Pochmann, Marcio. (2005). *O emprego na globalização*. São Paulo: Boitempo.

Project Management Institute. (2013a). *A Guide to the Project Management Body of Knowledge (PMBOK® Guide)*, 5th ed. Newtown Square, PA: PMI.

Project Management Institute. (2013b). *Managing Change in Organizations: A Practice Guide*. Newtown Square, PA: PMI.

Project Management Institute. (2014a). *Enabling Organizational Change through Strategic Initiatives*. Newtown Square, PA: PMI.

Project Management Institute. (2014b). *Pulse of the Profession®: The High Cost of Low Performance*. http://www.pmi.org/learning/thought-leadership/pulse/the-high-cost-of-low-performance-2014

Project Management Institute. (2014c). *Pulse of the Profession® In-Depth Report: Executive Sponsor Engagement—Top Driver of Project and Program Success*. https://www.pmi.org/learning/thought-leadership/pulse/top-driver-project-program-success

Project Management Institute. (2017). *Pulse of the Profession®: Success Rates Rise—Transforming the High Cost of Low Performance*. https://www.pmi.org/-/media/pmi/documents/public/pdf/learning/thought-leadership/pulse/pulse-of-the-profession-2017.pdf

Rabaglio, Maria Odete. (2008). *Gestão por competências*. Rio de Janeiro: Qualitymark.

Rad, Nader K., & Turley, Frank. (2015). *The Scrum Master Training Manual*. Management Plaza. https://mplaza.pm/downloads/Scrum%20Training%20Manual.pdf

Robbins, Stephen. (2002). *Comportamento organizacional* (9th ed.). (Reynaldo Marcondes, transl.). São Paulo: Prentice Hall.

Russell, Bertrand. (1956, 1992). *Lógica e conhecimento*. (Coleção os pensadores). São Paulo: Nova Cultural.

Schein, Edgar. (2010). *Organizational Culture and Leadership* (4th ed.). San Francisco: Jossey-Bass.

Schirato, Maria A. R. (2004). *O feitiço das organizações: Sistemas imaginários*. São Paulo: Atlas.

Selye, Hans. (1955). Stress and disease. *The Laryngoscope Journal* 65(7):500–514.

Senge, P. A. (2000). *Quinta disciplina: Caderno de campo*. Rio de Janeiro: Qualitymark.

Senge, P. A. (2002). *Quinta disciplina: Arte e prática da organização que aprende* (10th ed.). São Paulo: Editora Best Seller.

Shervington, Martin. (2005). *Coaching integral: Além do desenvolvimento pessoal*. (Neuza Simões, transl.). Rio de Janeiro: Qualitymark.

Simionato, Mônica, & Anderson, George. (2006). *Competências emocionais: O diferencial competitivo no trabalho*. Rio de Janeiro: Qualitymark.

Siqueira, Ethevaldo. (2004). *2015—Como viveremos: O futuro, na visão de 50 cientistas e futurologistas do Brasil e do Mundo* (2nd ed.). São Paulo: Saraiva.

Siqueira, M. M. M., & Gomide, S., Jr. (2004). Vínculos do indivíduo com a organização e com o trabalho. In: J. C. Zanelli, J. E. Borges-Andrade, & A. V. B. Bastos (eds.). *Psicologia, organizações e trabalho no Brasil*. Porto Alegre, Brazil: Artmed.

Stellman, Andrew, & Green, Jennifer. (2016). *Learning Agile: Understanding Scrum, XP, Lean, and Kanban* (2nd ed.). Sebastopol, CA: O'Reilly Media.

Terry, George R. (1977). *Principles of Management*. Halethorpe, MD: R. D. Irwin.

Vernon, M. D. (1973). *Motivação humana*. Petrópolis, Brazil: Vozes.

Wagner, J. A., III, & Hollenbeck, J. R. (1999). *Comportamento organizacional: Criando vantagem competitiva*. São Paulo: Saraiva.

Zook, Chris, & Allen, James. (2010). *Profit from the Core: A Return to Growth in Turbulent Times*. Boston, MA: Harvard Business Publishing.

Index

A

absenteeism, 141, 143
ACMP®. *See* Association of Change Management Professionals®
action plan, 23, 57–59, 67, 69, 83, 100–102, 130, 156
active communication, 119, 120, 157
affective domain, 180
agent(s) of change, 13, 28, 29, 62, 110, 113, 155, 161, 162, 170
agile methodologies, 19
align expectations, 61, 77, 81, 156
Allen, James, 165
antagonism, 7, 39, 45, 47, 58, 59, 65, 82, 117, 155, 160, 162
antagonistic behavior, 131, 157
antagonistic factors, 65, 155–157
antagonists, 16, 28, 29, 32, 35, 45, 65, 67, 92, 95–100, 108, 110, 127, 129–131, 143, 154, 155, 158, 160–162, 182
anthropology, 19
anticipatory grief, 6, 7, 49, 51, 64, 155, 156
assimilation, 27, 36, 53, 59, 111–113

Association of Change Management Professionals® (ACMP®), 3
attitudes and impulses, 154

B

Balanced Scorecard (BSC), 165
behavior, 2, 4–10, 13, 28, 29, 32, 34–36, 39–41, 46, 50–52, 58, 59, 61–63, 65, 69, 76, 79, 80, 95, 105, 111, 112, 115, 119, 125, 126, 130, 131, 133–135, 140, 141, 143, 144, 154–160, 163, 180, 181, 183, 184
behavior management, 4, 32, 95, 143
body language, 98, 131
brainstorming, 148–150, 152
briefing and debriefing sessions, 157, 163
BSC. *See* Balanced Scorecard
burnout syndrome, 141
business blueprint, 81
business plan, 26, 27, 29, 92, 111

C

causal relationship, 115

CEO. *See* chief executive officer

change and project management, 131

change leader, 82, 89, 107, 154, 179–181, 184

change management budget, 68

change management objective, 14

Change Management Office (CMO), 110, 165–177

change management process, 115

Change Management Strategic Plan, 23, 58, 63–68, 170, 175

change management team, 56, 58, 73, 87, 158, 170, 171, 173, 176

change manager, 3, 13, 30, 47, 53, 58, 85, 88, 110–112, 118, 120–122, 130, 134, 136–140, 142–144, 147, 152, 154, 158, 171, 173, 181–184

change process, 2, 8, 13, 24, 58, 69, 82, 83, 96, 112, 118, 166, 171, 179, 182

change sustainability, 58, 67, 90, 110, 113, 170

change sustainability phase, 170

change-sustaining strategy, 156

chief executive officer (CEO), 24, 100, 153, 166

closing phase, 58, 103

CMO. *See* Change Management Office

coaching and mentoring, 137, 144

cognitive domain, 180

communication, 2, 4, 7, 9, 13, 24, 25, 28, 30–32, 39–41, 43, 47, 48, 50, 58, 61, 62, 64–66, 69, 74, 79, 82, 84, 85, 88, 91–93, 100, 101, 112, 113, 116–124, 139, 140, 143, 146, 153, 157, 158, 160, 163, 166, 167, 182, 183

communication function, 118

communication planning, 40, 82, 117

companionship, 126, 127, 139, 143, 144

competencies for change leaders, 154, 179, 180

confidence, 55, 56, 65, 75, 82, 88, 90, 92, 96–99, 107, 126, 138, 143, 147, 152, 156, 157, 184

conflict, 4, 6, 13, 14, 24, 32, 41, 44, 48, 58, 60, 62, 69, 73, 74, 76, 79, 87, 91, 96, 112, 116, 122, 125, 126, 131, 133–138, 141, 143, 155, 156, 159, 161, 170, 173, 176, 180, 182, 183

contingency plan, 161

continuous improvement, 90, 112, 113

continuous organizational transformation process, 168

convergent thinking, 148, 150, 151

creative ideas, 145, 149

creative productivity, 9, 11, 141

creative/reflexive domain, 180

creativity, 4, 6, 11, 13, 41, 48, 58, 60, 69, 79, 105, 116, 138, 139, 145–148, 180, 183

credibility, 24, 38, 49, 54, 55, 61, 63, 65, 82, 108, 120, 137, 177, 180, 183, 184

cultural clash, 73, 74, 134

cultural fusion, 71

culture, 3, 11, 12, 14, 17, 22, 24–26, 28, 36–41, 43, 49, 51, 53, 54, 58, 59, 61, 63–67, 72–75, 77, 78, 84, 88, 89, 100, 103–105, 108, 110, 113, 118, 119, 121, 124, 134, 141, 143, 145, 146, 155, 157, 161, 162, 168–173, 175, 176

D

debriefing session, 61, 63, 107, 131, 157, 158, 163
decision-making power, 99, 129
decision-making stakeholder, 34, 35, 44, 97, 99, 100, 129–131
Delbecq, Andre, 150
delegation and opportunities for participation, 125
demobilization plan, 90, 104
difference between informing and communicating, 118
different perspectives, 32, 51, 130, 149, 163, 182
dimensions of communication, 118, 120
discomfort, 5, 6, 14, 17, 29, 46, 51, 59, 65, 74, 75, 89, 112, 113, 131, 158–160, 168, 175
distress, 30, 88, 107, 141, 154
divergent thinking, 148–151

E

ego, 25, 76, 125, 130, 133, 134, 160
ego clashes, 25, 76, 133, 134, 160
emotion, 30, 45, 54, 55, 62, 80, 102, 105, 121, 123, 124, 130, 131, 137, 140, 160, 181, 183
emotional reason, 130
empathic attitude, 30, 154, 180, 181
empathic communication, 13, 62
empathic position, 122
empathy, 154
engagement, 4, 11, 13, 16–18, 24, 25, 27, 29–32, 34, 35, 37, 39, 41, 44–47, 49–51, 55, 60, 63, 65, 69, 75, 81, 82, 88–92, 103–105, 107, 108, 111–113, 116–118, 121, 129, 139, 141, 143, 147, 153–160, 163, 167, 170, 171, 176, 179, 181–184
engagement factors, 63, 65, 82, 155, 156
enthusiasm, 54, 59–61, 84, 85, 89, 92, 97, 102, 105, 108, 111, 127, 139–141, 156–158, 180
enthusiasm of the leaders, 139, 140
entrepreneurial spirit, 145
equal treatment and attention to individual needs, 125
esteem, 138, 139
eustress, 141
execution phase, 4, 19, 20, 39, 42, 52, 56, 66, 75, 76, 79–81, 83, 88, 91, 92, 107, 110, 142, 154, 157, 163, 166
expectation, 2, 4, 24–26, 32, 34, 41, 49, 60, 61, 77, 80, 81, 89, 91, 103, 107, 112, 118, 125, 154–156, 158, 162, 163, 183, 184
explicit knowledge, 37, 103, 106
extraordinary communication, 122, 124
extraordinary (unplanned) communications, 82, 122
extreme measure, 160, 162, 163
extrinsic motivation, 138–140

F

face-to-face communication, 118, 158
factors of antagonism or engagement, 39
factors of resistance and antagonism, 82
fear, 6, 50, 62, 97, 118, 143, 154, 158
feedback, 43, 61–63, 80, 89, 97, 117–119, 121, 124, 154, 158, 163, 183

feedback channel, 43, 61, 97, 117, 119, 121, 124, 183
feelings and emotions, 181
focus on results, 180–182
frustration, 2, 50, 89, 103, 107, 157

G

Gaudêncio, Dr. Paulo, 11
good listener, 154, 180, 183
good practice, 14, 24, 32, 43, 46, 47, 50, 60, 64, 75, 85, 91, 92, 106, 118, 122, 131, 135, 158, 159, 165

H

Harvey, Jerry, 137
hasty implementation, 96, 100, 101
Heraclitus of Ephesus, 5
Herrmann, Ned, 62, 122, 123
high-performance team, 10, 49, 126
human beings, 6, 8, 10, 18, 54, 59, 160, 181
Human Change Management, 3, 19, 22, 181
human component, 2, 4, 110, 115
human factor, 1–4, 10, 11, 13–15, 41, 51, 52, 63, 65, 66, 72, 82, 86, 87, 96, 156, 166–168, 172, 175, 180–182
human factor management, 2–4, 13, 14, 63, 72
Human Resources, 1, 2, 4, 13, 39, 86, 89, 91, 108, 110, 118, 134, 137, 140, 144, 158, 162, 165, 171, 172

I

idea, 11, 72, 134, 137, 145, 147–152, 157

identity, 17, 29, 31, 32, 48, 61, 66, 126, 155
impacts of the change, 170
implementation decision meeting, 93, 98, 99, 101, 102, 157
imposed changes, 10, 11, 145, 161
inadequate behaviors, 143, 144, 159
indirect communication, 119
individual communication, 119, 121, 124, 183
individual position, 126
induced protagonism, 160, 161, 163
informal communication, 50, 118, 124, 163
innovation, 4, 13, 41, 60, 69, 105, 106, 145–147
innovation-oriented culture, 146
inspiring leader, 181
institutionalization, 36, 69, 91, 162
institutionalization of the change, 162
integrity, 180, 183, 184
interaction of people, 125
intrinsic motivation, 138–140, 180
intrinsic motivation and emotional intelligence, 180

J

Jarman, Beth, 145
journey of change, 101, 117

K

Kaplan, Robert S., 165
key success factor, 83
kick-off, 31, 60–63, 67, 79–81, 104, 127, 156, 171
knowledge assets, 84, 107
knowledge management, 56, 57, 73, 83, 85, 86, 90

knowledge manager, 57, 86, 106
knowledge repository, 85, 86, 106, 152
knowledge-sharing environment, 156
knowledge-sharing plan, 107
knowledge transfer, 90

L

Land, George, 145
layoff plan, 88
leader, 1, 2, 6, 13, 23, 25, 26, 28,
    29, 31, 32, 34, 36, 39–41, 44,
    49–56, 60, 64, 65, 76, 77, 82,
    85, 86, 88–90, 92, 97, 99, 103,
    107, 110, 111, 113, 124, 126,
    127, 139–141, 143, 144, 147,
    152, 154, 155, 157, 161–163,
    167–170, 177, 179–181, 184
leadership, 1, 14, 19, 40, 53, 55, 75,
    125, 134, 153, 155, 167, 172, 179
leadership styles, 55, 75, 134
learning management, 52, 83–85, 92,
    106
lessons learned, 105, 106
level of acceptance of stakeholders to
    change, 130
level of stress over the course of the
    project, 141
levels of maturity, 15, 53, 55, 64, 110,
    166–168, 172, 176
Lewin, Kurt, 2
logical conflicts, 134, 138, 159
logical issue, 112, 113, 131
long-term strategic relationship, 72

M

macro view of the methodology that
    is part of the HCMBOK®, 21
management of the stakeholders'
    engagement, 116

management plan, 57, 63, 156
managing the human factor in
    change processes, 166
Maslow, Abraham, 138
mass communication, 119, 120
maturity of the change management
    discipline, 176
maturity of the PMO, 172, 176
maturity of the strategy planning and
    execution process, 176
maturity to deal with loss, 52–55,
    134, 146
mobilizes the leaders, 29
moderator, 130, 131, 161
motivation, 4, 13, 28, 41, 44, 47, 50,
    51, 58, 60, 66, 69, 79, 81, 87,
    90, 95, 104, 107, 111, 112, 116,
    131, 133, 138–141, 147, 156,
    159, 180, 181
motivation and a positive
    environment, 131
mourning, 6, 88, 89, 111

N

negotiation, 10, 62, 71, 72, 134–137,
    182
negotiation styles, 135–137
NGT. *See* nominal group technique
nominal group technique (NGT),
    100, 150
Norton, David P., 165

O

Office of Strategy Management
    (OSM), 165
opinion maker, 35, 97, 127
ordinary communication, 66, 121,
    122, 124
organizational anticipatory grief, 6, 7

organizational change, 2–4, 6, 8, 13, 20, 23, 24, 26, 29, 44, 68, 71, 166, 168, 169, 172, 176, 179

organizational change management, 2–4, 13, 23, 26, 29, 44, 68, 166, 168, 172

organizational credibility, 49, 108

organizational culture, 14, 17, 22, 25, 26, 36–41, 43, 49, 53, 54, 58, 59, 61, 63, 65–67, 72, 74, 77, 78, 103, 104, 110, 113, 118, 121, 124, 134, 145, 155, 161, 168, 170–172, 176

organizational impact, 2, 28, 44, 65, 66, 81, 83, 87, 110, 156, 167, 170

organizational impact of the strategic initiatives, 170

organizational learning, 56, 105

organizational scar, 28, 141

organizational transformation, 14, 17, 18, 54, 110, 111, 157, 168, 173

OSM. *See* Office of Strategy Management

P

paradigm, 9, 36, 54, 60, 65, 145, 146, 148, 149, 168, 176, 180, 183

participatory approach, 31, 100

participatory changes, 11

participatory processes, 4, 13, 31, 37, 38, 41, 43, 45, 58, 69, 116, 129–131, 159

partnering environment, 74

passive communication, 119

people management, 19, 36, 40, 57, 86, 91, 172

people management processes, 36, 57, 86, 91

perception, 7, 8, 24, 28–30, 32, 37, 39, 40, 45–48, 52–55, 59, 62, 63, 65, 75, 76, 85, 89, 92, 110, 111, 118, 121, 123, 135, 136, 139, 147, 154, 155, 157–159, 161, 163, 176, 183

perception of "parenthood", 147, 159

personal agenda, 160

personal interest, 134

personality style, 127

personal style, 35, 54, 62, 133, 134, 140, 143

perspective, 17, 30, 32, 39, 51, 61, 108, 130, 133, 138, 139, 149, 154, 158, 163, 181, 182

persuasive tactic, 160, 161, 163

planning and initiation phase, 115

planning phase, 4, 12, 15, 17, 20, 28, 58, 63, 64, 67, 74, 75, 81, 83, 111, 117, 127, 142, 155, 167, 182

PMO. *See* Project Management Office

portfolio management, 168, 177

Portfolio Review Board, 170

positive project environment, 124, 143

post-project phase, 87, 107, 156

potential conflicts, 32, 76, 131, 133, 134, 137, 138, 155, 156, 173

presenteeism, 11, 80, 141, 143

Price, Dan, 153

production phase, 22, 35, 42, 58, 59, 66, 69, 83, 90, 91, 107–110, 115, 156, 157

project climate, 44, 73, 79, 87, 89, 111

project climate surveys, 111

project environment, 76, 88, 122, 124, 130, 133, 140, 143, 144, 152

project kick-off, 60, 61, 63, 67, 79, 104, 127, 156, 171

project management, 1, 3, 4, 13,

14, 17–20, 27, 30, 32, 36, 40,
43–48, 51–53, 56–58, 60, 61,
63, 64, 66–68, 76, 80, 81, 84,
87, 92, 96, 98–100, 105, 106,
110, 112, 119, 122, 131, 133,
154, 156, 158, 161, 166, 167,
170–172, 175, 176, 181
project management committee, 44,
45, 64, 67, 99, 112
Project Management Office (PMO),
106, 110, 156, 166–168,
170–177
project portfolio, 17, 166–168, 173
project team, 14, 27, 28, 31, 41–43,
45, 47–51, 58–62, 66, 69, 73,
75, 80–83, 86, 87, 90, 91, 95,
97, 101–105, 107, 111, 116, 119,
122, 129–131, 139, 140, 142,
154–158, 162, 163, 173, 182
protagonist, 161
psychological conflicts, 134, 159, 182
psychological insecurity, 49, 158, 168
psychological security, 7, 51, 75, 139,
155, 156
psychology, 2, 6, 7, 19
psychomotor domain, 180
*Pulse of the Profession® In-Depth
Report: Executive Sponsor
Engagement—Top Driver of
Project and Program Success*, 25
purpose, 4, 11, 12, 16, 17, 19, 20, 24,
25, 28–32, 35, 41, 43, 49, 50,
59–62, 64, 72, 77, 78, 81, 84,
105, 112, 117, 118, 120–122,
125, 126, 139, 140, 143, 155,
156, 158, 179–184

Q

quantitative and qualitative
indicators, 85

R

RACI Matrix, 41–43, 57, 61, 62, 66,
77, 91, 110, 120, 121, 126
readiness for change, 92, 96–101,
157
readiness indicators, 92
recognition plan, 67, 113
recurring activities, 115
recurring macro-activity, 116
reinforcing dynamics, 127
relationships, respect, and
cooperation, 127
repercussion, 110, 154
repetitive productivity, 9, 11
resilience, 7, 53, 54, 110, 179
resilient organization, 168
resistance, 4, 7, 16, 29, 30, 36, 37, 51,
54, 60, 62, 63, 65–67, 82, 87,
92, 96–98, 100, 111, 112, 117,
118, 131, 153, 154, 158, 159,
161–163, 168, 182
resistance-reinforcing factor, 129
retention plan, 73
Risk Map, 40, 41, 65, 86, 87, 92, 99,
101, 161
roles and responsibilities, 41, 42, 57,
60, 61, 66, 77, 84, 91, 110, 117,
118, 124, 134, 155, 156
root cause, 46, 80, 96, 112, 131, 135,
137, 138, 140, 144, 154, 159,
160, 163
rumor, 82, 122
Russell, Bertrand, 147

S

SCAMPER. *See* Substitute,
Combine, Adapt, Modify,
Put to another use, Eliminate,
Reorganize

seamless integration between the change management plan and the project, 156
self-actualization, 138
self-esteem, 127, 138, 161
self-realization, 104, 139
sellers of change, 29, 92, 100, 147
Selye, Hans, 141
sense of belonging, 31, 48, 126, 159
sensitivity, 6, 59, 89, 120–122, 134, 180, 181, 183
short-term goal, 127
silence, 122
social interaction, 62, 80, 126
social relations, 5, 127
sponsor, 4, 14, 16, 17, 24–26, 28–30, 32, 34–36, 44, 45, 47, 50, 55, 60, 61, 63, 64, 67, 76, 85, 92, 93, 97–102, 104, 108, 110, 112, 113, 120, 121, 130, 131, 134, 137, 153, 155, 161–163, 170, 177, 182
sponsorship, 24, 25, 39, 60, 64, 65, 110, 153, 155, 167, 176, 177
stakeholder engagement management, 24, 32, 41, 153
Stakeholder Map, 32, 33, 46, 53, 55, 57, 60, 61, 63–65, 67, 72, 82, 86, 87, 91, 92, 98, 99, 120, 121, 124, 129, 131, 154, 158, 163
state of belonging, 125
state of readiness for change, 96, 97, 99–101
steering committee, 44, 67, 85, 86, 99, 100, 122, 156, 161, 162
strategic challenges, 111
strategic initiative, 165, 168–170, 172
strategic objective, 1, 3, 4, 16, 17, 25–28, 52, 60, 72, 73, 109, 111,

112, 153, 167, 169, 172, 173, 176, 177
strategic plan, 15, 23, 26, 58, 63–68, 165, 166, 168, 170, 171, 175
strategic thinking and the ability to plan, 182
strategic vision, 68, 180, 182
strategy, 4, 5, 7, 9, 10, 12, 13, 15, 25, 29, 30, 32, 35, 37, 50, 51, 56–60, 63, 66, 67, 73, 80, 85, 89, 97–99, 101, 107, 110, 130, 136, 155–158, 160, 163, 165–173, 176, 177, 179, 182
stress, 13, 27, 28, 37, 41, 44, 48, 51, 56, 58, 69, 74, 79, 87, 95, 115, 116, 121, 126, 133, 141–143
stress tolerance, 116, 133
struggles for power, 134
Substitute, Combine, Adapt, Modify, Put to another use, Eliminate, Reorganize (SCAMPER), 148, 150–152
suggestion, 27, 67, 111, 123, 127, 152
survival instinct, 161
sustainability efforts, 110
sustainability of the change post-project, 81
sustaining of a change, 110

T

tacit knowledge, 56, 57
tactical management of change, 169
target audience, 83, 118, 122
team, 4, 9–11, 13, 14, 22, 25, 27, 28, 30–32, 34, 36, 40–69, 73–92, 95–107, 110, 111, 116, 119, 121, 122, 125–127, 129–131, 133, 137–147, 149, 151, 152, 154–159, 161–163, 168, 170, 171, 173, 176, 179–184

team spirit, 4, 11, 22, 40, 47, 48, 58,
    60, 62, 69, 77–79, 81, 95, 105,
    116, 125–127, 139, 143, 156
Terry, George R., 179
thanatology, 19
the vision of the organization's future
    state after the change, 26, 126
third generation of organizational
    change management, 2, 3
time schedule, 123, 129, 130
training plan, 51, 52, 74, 75, 86
trusting relationship, 154
types of project communication, 121

U

unilateral decision, 130
unresolved conflict, 137

V

vacation plan, 142
valley of despair, 15
Van de Ven, Andrew H., 150
veiled conflict, 126
vendor, 12, 27, 60, 61, 63, 71–78, 84,
    90, 92, 134, 181
virtual team, 47, 80, 130, 140, 158
vision of the future state, 28, 64, 78,
    167, 170
vision of the organization's future
    state, 26, 109, 125, 126, 153,
    162, 163, 167

Z

Zook, Chris, 165

Printed in the United States
by Baker & Taylor Publisher Services